UPDATED AND REVISED EDITION

Celebrate Recovery®

PARTICIPANT'S GUIDE
VOLUMES 5–8

THE JOURNEY CONTINUES

John Baker, along with his wife Cheryl, founded Celebrate Recovery®, a ministry started at Saddleback Church in 1991. John was on staff from the time Celebrate Recovery started until he went home to be with Jesus in 2021. He served as the Pastor of Membership, the Pastor of Ministries, and the Pastor of Saddleback Church's Signature Ministries. He also served as one of the nine Elder Pastors at Saddleback. John was a nationally known speaker and trainer in helping churches start Celebrate Recovery ministries. John's writing accomplishments include Celebrate Recovery's *The Journey Begins* Curriculum, *Life's Healing Choices*, the *Celebrate Recovery Study Bible* (general editor), and *The Landing* and *Celebration Place* (coauthor), *Your First Step to Celebrate Recovery* and *The Celebrate Recovery Daily Devotional* (coauthor). John and Cheryl were married for more than five decades and served together in Celebrate Recovery since the beginning. They have two adult children, Laura and Johnny, and five grandchildren.

Johnny Baker is the Global Executive Director of Celebrate Recovery, along with his wife Jeni. He has been on staff at Celebrate Recovery since 2004 and has been the Pastor of Celebrate Recovery at Saddleback Church since 2012. As an adult child of an alcoholic who chose to become an alcoholic himself, Johnny is passionate about breaking the cycle of dysfunction in his family and helping other families find the tools that will lead to healing and openness. He knows that because of Jesus Christ, and by continuing to stay active in Celebrate Recovery, Maggie, Chloe, and Jimmy—his three children—will never see him drink. Johnny is a nationally recognized speaker, trainer, and teacher of Celebrate Recovery. He is the author of *Road to Freedom*, a coauthor of the *Celebrate Recovery Daily Devotional*, *Celebration Place*, and *The Landing*, and is an associate editor of the *Celebrate Recovery Study Bible*. Johnny and Jeni have been married since 2000.

UPDATED AND REVISED EDITION

Celebrate Recovery®

PARTICIPANT'S GUIDE
VOLUMES 5–8

THE JOURNEY CONTINUES

A Program for Implementing a Christ-Centered Recovery Ministry in Your Church

JOHN BAKER & JOHNNY BAKER
FOREWORD BY RICK WARREN

Celebrate Recovery Participant's Guide, Volumes 5–8

©2016, 2025 by John Baker and Johnny Baker

Published in Grand Rapids, Michigan, by HarperChristian Resources. HarperChristian Resources is a registered trademark of HarperCollins Christian Publishing, Inc.

Requests for information should be sent to customercare@harpercollins.com.

ISBN 978-0-310-17600-8 (softcover)
ISBN 978-0-310-17599-5 (ebook)

All Scripture quotations are taken from the Holy Bible, New International Version®, NIV®. Copyright © 1973, 1978, 1984, 2011 by Biblica, Inc.® Used by permission. All rights reserved worldwide.

Any internet addresses (websites, blogs, etc.) and telephone numbers in this study guide are offered as a resource. They are not intended in any way to be or imply an endorsement by HarperChristian Resources, nor does HarperChristian Resources vouch for the content of these sites and numbers for the life of this study guide.

All rights reserved. No portion of this book may be reproduced, stored in a retrieval system, or transmitted in any form or by any means—electronic, mechanical, photocopy, recording, scanning, or other—except for brief quotations in critical reviews or articles, without the prior written permission of the publisher.

HarperChristian Resources titles may be purchased in bulk for church, business, fundraising, or ministry use. For information, please e-mail ResourceSpecialist@ChurchSource.com.

First Printing March 2025

Contents

Foreword by Rick Warren vii
The Road to Recovery ix
Twelve Steps and Their Biblical Comparisons x
Serenity Prayer xiii
Celebrate Recovery's Small Group Guidelines xv

Volume 5, Introduction 2
Volume 5, Lesson 1: Denial 3
Volume 5, Lesson 2: Power 9
Volume 5, Lesson 3: Hope 15
Volume 5, Lesson 4: Sanity 21
Volume 5, Lesson 5: Will 27
Volume 5, Lesson 6: Action 33
Volume 5, Congratulations and Your Next Step 38

Volume 6, Introduction 40
Volume 6, Lesson 7: Sponsor 41
Volume 6, Lesson 8: Truth 47
Volume 6, Lesson 9: Inventory 53
Volume 6, Lesson 10: Spiritual Inventory Part 1 65
Volume 6, Lesson 11: Spiritual Inventory Part 2 71
Volume 6, Congratulations and Your Next Step 77

THE JOURNEY CONTINUES

Volume 7, Introduction 80
Volume 7, Lesson 12: Confess 81
Volume 7, Lesson 13: Admit 87
Volume 7, Lesson 14: Ready 93
Volume 7, Lesson 15: Victory 99
Volume 7, Lesson 16: Amends 107
Volume 7, Lesson 17: Forgiveness 115
Volume 7, Lesson 18: Grace 121
Volume 7, Congratulations and Your Next Step 126

Volume 8, Introduction 128
Volume 8, Lesson 19: Habits 129
Volume 8, Lesson 20: Daily Inventory 135
Volume 8, Lesson 21: Relapse 141
Volume 8, Lesson 22: Gratitude 149
Volume 8, Lesson 23: Give 155
Volume 8, Lesson 24: Yes 161
Volume 8, Lesson 25: Leader 167
Volume 8, Congratulations and Your Next Step 173

Foreword by Rick Warren

The best known ministry at Saddleback Church—that is going to last for easily 100, maybe 200 years—started when a guy, who was a former drunk, came to me with a 13-page letter. And that ministry is called Celebrate Recovery®.

Now, let me just put this in perspective. This may be Saddleback's greatest contribution to the world. Over 20,000 people have completed the step studies at Saddleback's Celebrate Recovery. Over three and a half million people worldwide have gone through a Celebrate Recovery step study.

Right now, around the world, 27,000 churches are using Saddleback's ministry called Celebrate Recovery—27,000 churches! It is so successful that Celebrate Recovery is the official recovery program in 44 state and federal prison systems. It has been translated into 20 different languages.

Do you think John Baker, when he came to see me in my office many years ago and said, "I've got an idea for a ministry, Pastor Rick," imagined it would be affecting three and a half million people in 27,000 churches? No. You have no idea what God wants to do through you. You may have the next big ministry idea. You may have the next Celebrate Recovery dwelling in you—a ministry that could be started and reproduced to bless the whole world. One guy, out of his own pain, starts a ministry that now affects tens of thousands of churches and millions of people.

Dr. Rick Warren
Founder of Saddleback Church
(Excerpted from Pastor Warren's talk at Angel Stadium on
Saddleback's 35th anniversary, March 21, 2015)

The Road to Recovery

EIGHT PRINCIPLES BASED ON THE BEATITUDES

By Pastor Rick Warren

1. Realize I'm not God. I admit that I am powerless to control my tendency to do the wrong thing and that my life is unmanageable.
   Blessed are the poor in spirit, for theirs is the kingdom of heaven. (Matthew 5:3)
2. Earnestly believe that God exists, that I matter to Him, and that He has the power to help me recover.
   Blessed are those who mourn, for they will be comforted. (Matthew 5:4)
3. Consciously choose to commit all my life and will to Christ's care and control.
   Blessed are the meek, for they will inherit the earth. (Matthew 5:5)
4. Openly examine and confess my hurts, hang-ups, and habits to myself, to God, and to someone I trust.
   Blessed are the pure in heart, for they will see God. (Matthew 5:8)
5. Voluntarily submit to every change God wants to make in my life and humbly ask Him to remove my character defects.
   Blessed are those who hunger and thirst for righteousness, for they will be filled. (Matthew 5:6)
6. Evaluate all my relationships. Offer forgiveness to those who have hurt me and make amends for harm I've done to others, except when to do so would harm them or others.
   Blessed are the merciful, for they will be shown mercy. (Matthew 5:7)
   Blessed are the peacemakers, for they will be called children of God. (Matthew 5:9)
7. Reserve a daily time with God for self-examination, Bible reading, and prayer in order to know God and His will for my life and to gain the power to follow His will.
8. Yield myself to God to be used to bring this Good News to others, both by my example and by my words.
   Blessed are those who are persecuted because of righteousness, for theirs is the kingdom of heaven. (Matthew 5:10)

Twelve Steps and Their Biblical Comparisons[1]

1. We admitted we were powerless over our addictions and compulsive behaviors, that our lives had become unmanageable.

    For I know that good itself does not dwell in me, that is, in my sinful nature. For I have the desire to do what is good, but I cannot carry it out. (Romans 7:18)

2. We came to believe that a power greater than ourselves could restore us to sanity.

    For it is God who works in you to will and to act in order to fulfill his good purpose. (Philippians 2:13)

3. We made a decision to turn our lives and our wills over to the care of God.

    Therefore, I urge you, brothers and sisters, in view of God's mercy, to offer your bodies as a living sacrifice, holy and pleasing to God—this is your true and proper worship. (Romans 12:1)

4. We made a searching and fearless moral inventory of ourselves.

    Let us examine our ways and test them, and let us return to the LORD. (Lamentations 3:40)

5. We admitted to God, to ourselves, and to another human being the exact nature of our wrongs.

    Therefore confess your sins to each other and pray for each other so that you may be healed. (James 5:16)

6. We were entirely ready to have God remove all these defects of character.

    Humble yourselves before the Lord, and he will lift you up. (James 4:10)

---

1. Throughout this material, you will notice several references to the Christ-centered 12 Steps. Our prayer is that Celebrate Recovery will create a bridge to the millions of people who are familiar with the secular 12 Steps (I acknowledge the use of some material from the 12 Suggested Steps of Alcoholics Anonymous.) and in so doing, introduce them to the one and only true Higher Power, Jesus Christ. Once they begin that relationship, asking Christ into their hearts as Lord and Savior, true healing and recovery can begin!

7. We humbly asked Him to remove all our shortcomings.

    If we confess our sins, he is faithful and just and will forgive us our sins and purify us from all unrighteousness. (1 John 1:9)

8. We made a list of all persons we had harmed and became willing to make amends to them all.

    Do to others as you would have them do to you. (Luke 6:31)

9. We made direct amends to such people whenever possible, except when to do so would injure them or others.

    "Therefore, if you are offering your gift at the altar and there remember that your brother or sister has something against you, leave your gift there in front of the altar. First go and be reconciled to them; then come and offer your gift." (Matthew 5:23–24)

10. We continued to take personal inventory and when we were wrong, promptly admitted it.

    *So, if you think you are standing firm, be careful that you don't fall!
    (1 Corinthians 10:12)*

11. We sought through prayer and meditation to improve our conscious contact with God, praying only for knowledge of His will for us and power to carry that out.

    Let the message of Christ dwell among you richly. (Colossians 3:16)

12. Having had a spiritual experience as the result of these steps, we try to carry this message to others and to practice these principles in all our affairs.

    Brothers and sisters, if someone is caught in a sin, you who live by the Spirit should restore that person gently. But watch yourselves, or you also may be tempted. (Galatians 6:1)

Serenity Prayer

If you have attended secular recovery programs, you have seen the first four lines of the "Prayer for Serenity." The following is the complete prayer. I encourage you to pray it daily as you work through the principles!

Prayer for Serenity

God, grant me the serenity
to accept the things I cannot change,
the courage to change the things I can,
and the wisdom to know the difference.
Living one day at a time,
enjoying one moment at a time;
accepting hardship as a pathway to peace; taking, as Jesus did,
this sinful world as it is,
not as I would have it;
trusting that You will make all things right
if I surrender to Your will;
so that I may be reasonably happy in this life and supremely happy with You forever in
     the next. Amen.

Reinhold Niebuhr

Celebrate Recovery's Small Group Guidelines

The following five guidelines will ensure that your small group is a safe place. They need to be read at the beginning of every meeting.

1. Keep your sharing focused on your own thoughts and feelings using "I" and "me" statements. Limit your sharing to three to five minutes.
2. There is NO cross talk. Cross talk is when two individuals engage in conversation excluding all others. Each person is free to express his or her feelings without interruptions.
3. We are here to support one another, not "fix" one another.
4. Anonymity and confidentiality are basic requirements. What is shared in the group stays in the group. The only exception is when someone threatens to injure themselves or others.
5. Offensive language has no place in a Christ-centered recovery group.

The following guidelines are to be used in all online Open Share Groups and Step studies.

6. **All members must use headphones.** This will ensure that no one else can overhear what is shared in the group.
7. **All members must be on camera and alone in the room,** with the camera facing them the whole time. If the group leader asks, they must show the rest of the group that no one else is in the room.
8. **The meetings will not be recorded.** This protects the confidentiality and anonymity of the meetings.

Emphasize at the close of your meeting that Guidelines stay intact as participants fellowship with each other after the meeting.

VOLUME 5

Moving Forward in God's Grace

THE JOURNEY CONTINUES

Introduction

See, I am doing a new thing! Now it springs up; do you not perceive it? (Isaiah 43:19)

Welcome to *The Journey Continues*!

We are so excited for you as you continue to grow on the road to recovery! If you are starting *The Journey Continues*, it means a few things about you. First, it means you are ready to take the next step on your recovery journey and take your recovery to the next level. It also means that you have already completed at least one *The Journey Begins* (the original Celebrate Recovery® Participant's Guide, Volumes 1–4) step study group. Last, it means that you have had some time, probably at least six months since completing that study, to begin applying the Biblical Principles of Recovery to your life.

Here in *The Journey Continues* you will build on what you learned about Christ and yourself in *The Journey Begins*, grow deeper in your faith, and strengthen your recovery. You'll find brand new acrostics, new questions, and of course, hundreds of Bible verses. Just as in *The Journey Begins*, you'll grow closer to Christ and the other members of your group as you dig deeper into your life and find freedom in new areas.

To begin *The Journey Continues*, you will see if DENIAL has snuck back into your life in any way and, if so, what to do about it. Since you learned what you give up when you admitted your powerlessness in *The Journey Begins*, here you will explore what God's POWER can do in your life and will see how keeping your HOPE in God can maintain your SANITY. Because you have already turned your life over to Christ, in or before you completed Principle 3 of *The Journey Begins*, you will focus here on the daily ACTIONS you need to take to turn your WILL to Him.

Make sure you take the time to write out your answers before you meet with your group each week. The more you put in to this study, the more you'll get out of it. We will be praying for you as you continue your recovery journey.

"The Lord makes firm the steps of the one who delights in him; though he may stumble, he will not fall, for the Lord upholds him with his hand" (Psalm 37:23–24).

In His steps,
John Baker
Johnny Baker

LESSON 1

Denial

Principle 1: Realize I'm not God. I admit that I am powerless to control my tendency to do the wrong thing and that my life is unmanageable.

Blessed are the poor in spirit, for theirs is the kingdom of heaven. (Matthew 5:3)

Step 1: We admitted we were powerless over our addictions and compulsive behaviors, that our lives had become unmanageable.

For I know that good itself does not dwell in me, that is, in my sinful nature. For I have the desire to do what is good, but I cannot carry it out. (Romans 7:18)

Please begin your time together by reading "The First Step, Day 1" of the *Celebrate Recovery Daily Devotional.*

As we begin *The Journey Continues*, we each need to start off by answering this one question: "Have I put on the mask of denial again?"

Before you can make any further progress in this exciting new step study, you need to face your denial. It doesn't matter how long you have been in recovery—you may have been working the steps and principles for years—denial can rear its ugly head and return at any time! You may trade addictions, begin new compulsive behaviors, or be on the road to relapse without even knowing it. By removing your mask of denial, you can take your recovery to the next level, or your recovery can even begin again! Even if you feel that you haven't actively stepped back into denial, denial is something you must be on guard against.

We need to begin *The Journey Continues* by searching our hearts to see if we have allowed any denial back into our recovery. So let's get this new exciting journey started!

DENIAL

D—Disrupts our progress in our recoveries

Hiding our feelings, returning to denial, freezes our recovery and binds our progress.

Be diligent in these matters; give yourself wholly to them, so that everyone may see your progress. (1 Timothy 4:15)

Would not God have discovered it, since he knows the secrets of the heart? (Psalm 44:21)

E—Enables old hurts, hang-ups, and habits to return

As we continue to go through this program, we learn that it is only in the present that positive change can occur. The return of old hurts, hang-ups, and habits makes us unable to live and enjoy God's plans for us in the present.

As a dog returns to its vomit, so fools repeat their folly. (Proverbs 26:11)

DENIAL

N—Negatively affects the repair work we have done on our relationships

As we slip back into denial, we again start to isolate from those close to us. We start to destroy the new trust and fellowship we have been given by them.

My friends and companions avoid me because of my wounds; my neighbors stay far away. (Psalm 38:11)

All this I saw, as I applied my mind to everything done under the sun. There is a time when a man lords it over others to his own hurt. (Ecclesiastes 8:9)

> The guilty man is the one who wants to be alone; the man who is right with God does not. . . . The final curse of a disobedient soul is that it becomes a separate, self-conscious individual.
>
> —OSWALD CHAMBERS

I—Interrupts our daily walk with God

As we slip further into our denial, it is harder for us to maintain our closeness to God. We think we are fooling everyone, even God. But we are only fooling ourselves.

Anyone who runs ahead and does not continue in the teaching of Christ does not have God; whoever continues in the teaching has both the Father and the Son. (2 John 1:9)

"Whoever is not with me is against me, and whoever does not gather with me scatters." (Luke 11:23)

A—Allows risk of possible relapse

As we decrease our closeness to God and others, the more we increase the chance of relapse.

This is what the LORD says: "Stand at the crossroads and look; ask for the ancient paths, ask where the good way is, and walk in it, and you will find rest for your souls. But you said, 'We will not walk in it.' " (Jeremiah 6:16)

L—Loss of valuable time

The longer we keep our denial hidden, the more time we are wasting that could be spent on continuing to grow. We need to ask God to help us break free from our denial and continue our forward journey in recovery.

Therefore, since we are surrounded by such a great cloud of witnesses, let us throw off everything that hinders and the sin that so easily entangles. And let us run with perseverance the race marked out for us. (Hebrews 12:1)

If anyone, then, knows the good they ought to do and doesn't do it, it is sin for them. (James 4:17)

The greatest wasteland in all of our earth . . . our waste of the time that God has given us each day.

—BILLY GRAHAM

Questions for Reflection and Discussion

1. Have you noticed that your recovery has been stalled? In what ways has your joy and serenity faded? Describe in detail.

2. Have you begun to believe that you have control over certain aspects of your life? If so, which ones?

DENIAL

3. Have any of your old hurts, hang-ups, or habits begun to fill your mind? (Ask your sponsor or accountability partners if they have seen any old or new negative patterns emerging in you.)

4. Have you begun to struggle with or lost any of your important relationships? List each of them and describe the struggle.

5. In the last six months, have you grown closer to or farther away from God? Describe why you think it has changed.

6. As completely as you can, describe your relationship with God today.

7. Have you been having any thoughts of "the good old days"? Any thoughts that you can handle your struggles differently this time? Write down the specific thoughts you have been having.

8. List some of the tools that help you from slipping back into denial. Are you using them?

9. How do you continue to use your time to help newcomers? How do you help ensure others that they are not stuck in denial? (Be specific; everyone in your group will benefit from your answers.)

PRAYER

God, thank You for this time together. Thank You for everyone here today. Lord, we ask You to examine our hearts to see if we have allowed any denial back into our recoveries. If we have and we can't see it, open our eyes so we can expose it to Your light.

As we join together, as our journey continues, help us grow closer to You and to one another. It is in Your Son's precious name we pray. Amen.

LESSON 2

Power

Principle 1: Realize I'm not God. I admit that I am powerless to control my tendency to do the wrong thing and that my life is unmanageable.

Blessed are the poor in spirit, for theirs is the kingdom of heaven. (Matthew 5:3)

Step 1: We admitted we were powerless over our addictions and compulsive behaviors, that our lives had become unmanageable.

I know that good itself does not dwell in me, that is, in my sinful nature. For I have the desire to do what is good, but I cannot carry it out. (Romans 7:18)

Please begin your time together by reading "Casting Anxiety, Day 12" from the *Celebrate Recovery Daily Devotional*.

In Lesson 2 of *The Journey Begins*, we looked at the "serenity robbers" we would give up when we admitted we were powerless. By admitting our powerlessness, we find that there is a true Higher Power, whose name is Jesus, who can and will restore us to sanity. And He can do so much more!

You are either going to serve God or self. You can't do both! Matthew 6:24 says, "No one can serve two masters. Either you will hate the one and love the other, or you will be devoted to the one and despise the other. You cannot serve both God and money." Another term for serving "ourselves" is serving the "flesh." Flesh is the Bible's word for our unperfected human nature, our sin nature.

If you leave the "h" off the end of flesh and reverse the remaining letters, you spell the word *self*. Flesh is the self-life. It is what we are when we are left to our own devices. When our "self" is out of control, all attempts at control—of self or others—fail. In fact, our attempt to control ourselves and others is what got us into trouble in the first place. To have long-lasting peace in your life, God needs to be the one in control.

Because you now have a relationship with Jesus, you now have the POWER to overcome any hurt, hang-up, or habit. Let's look at what that power can do in your life.

POWER

P—Peace of mind can be found

Instead of having our minds racing, trying to keep all of the plates spinning, we can now enjoy the peace of mind that God offers. Then we can turn from trying to do things on our own power and rely on His instead.

> *And the peace of God, which transcends all understanding, will guard your hearts and your minds in Christ Jesus. (Philippians 4:7)*

> *Now may the Lord of peace himself give you peace at all times and in every way. The Lord be with all of you. (2 Thessalonians 3:16)*

O—Overcoming temptation is possible

Once it may have felt that temptation was impossible to resist. Now that we have God's power, we have the ability to look for ways to escape temptation before giving in.

No temptation has overtaken you except what is common to mankind. And God is faithful; he will not let you be tempted beyond what you can bear. But when you are tempted, he will also provide a way out so that you can endure it. (1 Corinthians 10:13)

So I say, walk by the Spirit, and you will not gratify the desires of the flesh. (Galatians 5:16)

W—Worrying can stop

Worry happens when we face a problem bigger than ourselves. When we know that we can't solve a problem with our own power, or when we fear that we will be overcome by something we can't handle, we worry. However, when we trust God and plug into His power through prayer, we find we can stop worrying because nothing is too big for God to handle.

Therefore do not worry about tomorrow, for tomorrow will worry about itself. Each day has enough trouble of its own. (Matthew 6:34)

Those who know your name trust in you, for you, Lord, have never forsaken those who seek you. (Psalm 9:10)

E—Every character defect can be healed

There's no issue that God can't heal. Even after completing a step study, we may be holding onto things we have been unwilling to face. We may have some hurts we are afraid to hand over to God, or a secondary recovery issue that we have not dealt with. We now have the power to face them because of God's power. There isn't a character defect or issue in the world that God can't heal!

He heals the brokenhearted and binds up their wounds. (Psalm 147:3)

R—Real relationships can be formed

Denial and the refusal to admit we have had problems caused us to lose or damage many of our relationships in the past. Coming out of denial, and admitting we are powerless, gives us the ability to stop trying to act like we have it all together and form true trust and intimacy with others.

For just as each of us has one body with many members, and these members do not all have the same function, so in Christ we, though many, form one body, and each member belongs to all the others. (Romans 12:4–5)

And let us consider how we may spur one another on toward love and good deeds, not giving up meeting together, as some are in the habit of doing, but encouraging one another—and all the more as you see the Day approaching. (Hebrews 10:24–25)

Questions for Reflection and Discussion

1. Have you fully admitted your powerlessness over your life's hurts, hang-ups, and habits? If not, what's holding you back?

2. How have you experienced "the peace of God, which transcends all understanding"? Share details.

3. How are you plugging into God's power when you are stressed?

4. Share a time when you have felt God's power help you overcome a temptation. Be specific.

5. Sharing a victory over temptation with a newcomer is so important! Who do you know that would be encouraged by hearing that story?

6. What are you worried about today? How can you turn that worry over to God?

7. Now that you've been in recovery for a while, what character defects are you planning on focusing on during *The Journey Continues*?

8. Have you been holding back a particular hurt, hang-up, or habit that you are now ready to face? If so, what is it?

9. Question 6 of the POWERLESS lesson in Participant's Guide 1, *The Journey Begins* asks, "How has your denial isolated you from your important relationships?" Have you seen any change in those relationships since your involvement in Celebrate Recovery? If so, what has happened? If not, why not?

10. What healthy, real relationships have you formed in Celebrate Recovery, and how have they helped your recovery journey?

PRAYER

Dear God, please continue to give me the power to overcome my hurts, hang-ups, and habits. I know I need to stop pretending I have it all under control, and that I need to rely on Your power. Help me overcome temptations and worry, and allow me to lean on the people You have placed in my life. Amen.

LESSON 3

Hope

Principle 2: Earnestly believe that God exists, that I matter to Him, and that He has the power to help me recover.

Blessed are those who mourn, for they will be comforted. (Matthew 5:4)

Step 2: We came to believe that a power greater than ourselves could restore us to sanity.

For it is God who works in you to will and to act in order to fulfill his good purpose. (Philippians 2:13)

Please begin your time together by reading "The Second Step, Day 30" from the *Celebrate Recovery Daily Devotional.*

In the *The Journey Begins* step study, we learned that HOPE is being open to change. However, some of us were afraid to change, even if our past was very painful. We resisted change because of our fear of the unknown, or, in our despair, we thought we didn't deserve anything better.

Here's the good news: Hope opens doors where despair closes them! Hope discovers what *can* be done instead of grumbling about what *can't* be done.

We understand throughout our lives that we will continue to encounter hurts and trials that we are powerless to change, but with God's help, we can be open to allow those circumstances and situations to change us—to make us better, not bitter.

Ephesians 4:23 gives us a challenge to that end: "Be made new in the attitude of your minds."

However, as the months and years have passed since your last step study, you might have slowly confused or forgotten where your true, lasting Hope comes from. Sadly, the farther we get from the early days of our recovery, the more we can begin to forget or minimize the people and tools that allowed us to get where we are today. One of the major things we can minimize is just how important our total surrender to God was and is.

HOPE

H—Hope comes from God

We cannot have continued healing from our hurts, hang-ups, and habits without hope. Real hope can only come from God. If we place our hope in people or things, we will come up empty. But when we trust in God, our hope is secure.

Hopes placed in mortals die with them; all the promise of their power comes to nothing. (Proverbs 11:7)

Yes, my soul, find rest in God; my hope comes from him. (Psalm 62:5)

May the God of hope fill you with all joy and peace as you trust in him, so that you may overflow with hope by the power of the Holy Spirit. (Romans 15:13)

O—Open our hearts to allow God to restore all our hope in Him

If we are feeling hopeless, it may be that we have closed our hearts to God. God will not force His love or hope on us. In order for hope to be restored in our lives, we need to open ourselves and invite Him to work in us.

Why, my soul, are you downcast? Why so disturbed within me? Put your hope in God, for I will yet praise him, my Savior and my God. (Psalm 42:5)

When anxiety was great within me, your consolation brought me joy. (Psalm 94:19)

P—Purpose for our life is found in Christ's hope

When we discover our purpose, serving God and others, we are filled with hope!

However, as it is written: "What no eye has seen, what no ear has heard, and what no human mind has conceived"—the things God has prepared for those who love him. (1 Corinthians 2:9)

But I have raised you up for this very purpose, that I might show you my power and that my name might be proclaimed in all the earth. (Exodus 9:16)

> Everywhere I go I find that people . . . both leaders and individuals . . . are asking one basic question, "Is there any hope for the future?" My answer is the same, "Yes, through Jesus Christ."
>
> **—BILLY GRAHAM**

E—Expect and hope for continued new growth and victories

This study is called *The Journey Continues* for a reason—God isn't finished with us yet. We have more change and victory to come!

Be joyful in hope, patient in affliction, faithful in prayer. (Romans 12:12)

Now faith is confidence in what we hope for and assurance about what we do not see. (Hebrews 11:1)

THE JOURNEY CONTINUES

Questions for Reflection and Discussion

1. Today, where is your hope found: in Christ or in someone or something of this world? Why?

2. Summarize just how hopeful in Christ you felt in those early days of recovery. Then write a brief paragraph on how that has changed today. (Has it grown or declined? Why?)

3. What is something that you are discouraged about today? Be specific.

4. Is there anything that you are doubting about your relationship with God today? Again, be specific.

5. What have you discovered as God's purpose for your life?

6. How are you doing at living out that purpose you described in question 5? And with whom have you shared your purpose: someone who could encourage and be objective with you?

7. What are some of the victories you have celebrated by not losing hope?

8. Describe your last experience of sharing the hope found in Christ with a newcomer. (Be specific; everyone in your group will benefit from your answer.)

PRAYER

God, Your Word says, "May the God of hope fill you with all joy and peace as you trust in him, so that you may overflow with hope by the power of the Holy Spirit."[1]

God, You are our hope, and that hope is given to us through Your unconditional love for each of us. We pray that we never take it for granted. Help us to share it with others, especially newcomers. Please, God, help us to do this in every opportunity we are given. Amen.

---

1. Romans 15:13

LESSON
4

Sanity

Principle 2: Earnestly believe that God exists, that I matter to Him, and that He has the power to help me recover.

Blessed are those who mourn, for they will be comforted. (Matthew 5:4)

Step 2: We came to believe that a power greater than ourselves could restore us to sanity.

For it is God who works in you to will and to act in order to fulfill his good purpose. (Philippians 2:13)

Please begin your time together by reading "Walk This Way, Day 24" from the *Celebrate Recovery Daily Devotional.*

In Principle 2, we learn how a relationship with Jesus can restore us to SANITY. We defined *sanity* in *The Journey Begins* as a wholeness of mind and spirit. As our recovery journeys continue, we will have times and issues that will try to rob us of that sanity. Even though we are changing, the people and situations around us may not be. In fact, the people in our lives may not even be supportive of our changes. No matter what our situation, we can find the wholeness of mind that we are looking for.

Now that we have that hope, and are continuing to be restored, how do we maintain our sanity?

SANITY

S—Steady growth, not perfection, is the goal

One way to lose our sanity is to look for perfection or complete immediate change. It takes time to overcome our hurts, hang-ups, and habits. Instead of looking for perfection, we need to be on the lookout for all of the small ways we or our loved ones have changed.

Being confident of this, that he who began a good work in you will carry it on to completion until the day of Christ Jesus. (Philippians 1:6)

Not that I have already obtained all this, or have already arrived at my goal, but I press on to take hold of that for which Christ Jesus took hold of me. Brothers and sisters, I do not consider myself yet to have taken hold of it. But one thing I do: Forgetting what is behind and straining toward what is ahead, I press on toward the goal to win the prize for which God has called me heavenward in Christ Jesus. (Philippians 3:12–14)

> We all want progress, but if you're on the wrong road, progress means doing an about-turn and walking back to the right road; in that case, the man who turns back soonest is the most progressive.
>
> —C. S. LEWIS

SANITY

A—Accept the things I cannot change

The Serenity Prayer reminds us to ask God for the "serenity to accept the things I cannot change." It's in this "accepting" that we are able to remind ourselves that there are things we need to do. Then there are things that only God can do. When we allow God to handle the things we cannot change, we will keep our sanity.

In peace I will lie down and sleep, for you alone, Lord, make me dwell in safety. (Psalm 4:8)

Even though I walk through the darkest valley, I will fear no evil, for you are with me; your rod and your staff, they comfort me. (Psalm 23:4)

Cast all your anxiety on him because he cares for you. (1 Peter 5:7)

N—Notice new hurts, hang-ups, and habits, and take action

If we've been in recovery for a while and still feel as if our life is out of control, it may be that we have issues we have not yet dealt with. It might even be a new issue that started after attending Celebrate Recovery. Whether new issues or unresolved ones from an earlier step study, until they are dealt with, they will cause us to spin out of control.

But you, man of God, flee from all this, and pursue righteousness, godliness, faith, love, endurance and gentleness. (1 Timothy 6:11)

Then I acknowledged my sin to you and did not cover up my iniquity. I said, "I will confess my transgressions to the Lord." And you forgave the guilt of my sin. (Psalm 32:5)

I—Invite others to help us along the way

One of the most powerful tools we can use to protect our recovery and our sanity is other people. We all must invite other people to hold us accountable and keep us on track. These people have the ability to look into our lives and see things we may not notice on our own.

Two are better than one, because they have a good return for their labor: If either of them falls down, one can help the other up. But pity anyone who falls and has no one to help them up. . . . Though one may be overpowered, two can defend themselves. A cord of three strands is not quickly broken. (Ecclesiastes 4:9–10, 12)

And let us consider how we may spur one another on toward love and good deeds, not giving up meeting together, as some are in the habit of doing, but encouraging one another—and all the more as you see the Day approaching. (Hebrews 10:24–25)

T—Try to keep short accounts

While healthy people can help keep us on track, unhealthy relationships can derail us. It would be nice to think that we will never again be hurt by others, but it isn't realistic. While we can't control other people and keep them from hurting us, we can control our response. Instead of holding onto grudges or keeping score, we can extend forgiveness, and make amends, quickly.

"In your anger do not sin": Do not let the sun go down while you are still angry. (Ephesians 4:26)

Get rid of all bitterness, rage and anger, brawling and slander, along with every form of malice. Be kind and compassionate to one another, forgiving each other, just as in Christ God forgave you. (Ephesians 4:31–32)

Y—Your Higher Power is on your side!

Remember that you are not alone! Not only do you have the other people sitting in this group with you, but you also have the God who created the universe on your side! You are not alone!

For God did not appoint us to suffer wrath but to receive salvation through our Lord Jesus Christ. (1 Thessalonians 5:9)

No temptation has overtaken you except what is common to mankind. And God is faithful; he will not let you be tempted beyond what you can bear. But when you are tempted, he will also provide a way out so that you can endure it. (1 Corinthians 10:13)

For he has rescued us from the dominion of darkness and brought us into the kingdom of the Son he loves, in whom we have redemption, the forgiveness of sins. (Colossians 1:13–14)

SANITY

Questions for Reflection and Discussion

1. Since first completing *The Journey Begins* step study, how has your life moved from chaos to hope?

2. What are some steady improvements you have seen in your recovery? Be specific. And how can focusing on these improvements help you keep your sanity?

3. What are some things going on, right now, that are out of your control? Again, be specific.

4. How can you give the things you mentioned in question 3 to Christ? (Write down how giving out-of-control situations to Christ helped you in the past.)

5. Have you noticed any new hurts, hang-ups, or habits since you started recovery? Be specific. If so, what action(s) have you taken to deal with them?

6. Who have you invited to help you on your journey?

7. Share about a time you helped someone else when they needed encouragement in their recovery.

8. How can making amends or quickly offering forgiveness help you keep your sanity? List some examples.

9. How does knowing Jesus is on your side help you in your recovery?

PRAYER

Dear God, thank You for helping us make decisions based on Your truth. Today, we can live our lives knowing that we can always put our hope in You. When we face a new struggle, we can turn it over to You. When we need to offer our amends to others, we can do so modeling Your love for us. We pray that others will see more of You and less of us as we continue to grow in our journey. In Your Son's precious name we pray, amen.

LESSON 5

Will

Principle 3: Consciously choose to commit all my life and will to Christ's care and control.

Blessed are the meek, for they will inherit the earth. (Matthew 5:5)

Step 3: We made a decision to turn our lives and our wills over to the care of God.

Therefore, I urge you, brothers and sisters, in view of God's mercy, to offer your bodies as a living sacrifice, holy and pleasing to God—this is your true and proper worship. (Romans 12:1)

THE JOURNEY CONTINUES

Please begin your time together by reading "The Third Step, Day 60" from the *Celebrate Recovery Daily Devotional*.

In *The Journey Begins* step study, Lesson 5's acrostic is TURN. That is the most important decision we will ever make. But after we decide to turn our lives over to Christ as our Higher Power, Lord and Savior, the next step is to understand and follow God's WILL for our lives. That is a daily, sometimes hourly process. Relying solely on our own understanding is what got most of us into recovery in the first place! Many of us tried to fill God's role and came up empty and broken.

> The greatest barrier to knowing God's will is simply that we want to run our own lives. Our problem is that a battle is going on in our hearts—a battle between our wills and God's will.
> —BILLY GRAHAM

After making the decision to ask Jesus into our lives, we must begin to seek His will in all our decisions. We need to get to know and understand Him and what He wants for our lives. Proverbs 3:5–6 says, "Trust in the Lord with all your heart and lean not on your own understanding; in all your ways submit to him, and he will make your paths straight."

Our understanding is earthbound. It's human to the core. Limited. Finite. We operate in a dimension totally unlike that of our Lord. He knows no such limitations. We understand now that God sees forever!

Someday, we will see Jesus face-to-face. The fog of interpretation will be lifted, and our understanding will be perfected. Praise God that we do not need a perfect understanding of Him to ask Jesus into our lives as our Lord and Savior! But we do need to be continuously growing in Christ thereafter.

For now we see only a reflection as in a mirror; then we shall see face to face. Now I know in part; then I shall know fully, even as I am fully known. (1 Corinthians 13:12)

WILL

W—Will is to "Consciously choose to commit all my life and will to Christ's care and control." (Principle 3)

Blessed are the meek, for they will inherit the earth. (Matthew 5:5)

Will is the second part of Principle 3. We exchange our will for His. This is a choice we make daily—it won't happen on its own.

So I say, walk by the Spirit, and you will not gratify the desires of the flesh. For the flesh desires what is contrary to the Spirit, and the Spirit what is contrary to the flesh. They are in conflict with each other, so that you are not to do whatever you want. (Galatians 5:16–17)

Therefore let us move beyond the elementary teachings about Christ and be taken forward to maturity. (Hebrews 6:1)

I—Initial decision to accept Christ as your Lord and Savior is a one-time decision that you made during your (or before you began) *The Journey Begins* **step study**

And you also were included in Christ when you heard the message of truth, the gospel of your salvation. When you believed, you were marked in him with a seal, the promised Holy Spirit. (Ephesians 1:13)

But grow in the grace and knowledge of our Lord and Savior Jesus Christ. To him be glory both now and forever! Amen. (2 Peter 3:18)

L—Look for God's will in all our decisions. No matter how large or small

Sometimes we believe that God only cares about the big-picture things, but God's will extends to all areas of our lives. We need to seek Him in every decision.

Do not conform to the pattern of this world, but be transformed by the renewing of your mind. Then you will be able to test and approve what God's will is—his good, pleasing and perfect will. (Romans 12:2)

He made known to us the mystery of his will according to his good pleasure, which he purposed in Christ. (Ephesians 1:9)

L—Listen and pray for God's will prior to making our decisions. Share them with our accountability team before making any major decisions

Instead, you ought to say, "If it is the Lord's will, we will live and do this or that." As it is, you boast in your arrogant schemes. All such boasting is evil. If anyone, then, knows the good they ought to do and doesn't do it, it is sin for them. (James 4:15–17)

A sluggard is wiser in his own eyes than seven people who answer discreetly. (Proverbs 26:16)

Questions for Reflection and Discussion

1. Since making the decision to follow Christ, how are you continuously learning to grow in Christ? Share details.

2. Why is it important to include God in all your big and small decisions? List at least three reasons.

3. How does it feel when you are living in God's purpose, His will, for your life? List at least three benefits.

WILL

4. How does it feel when you find yourself out of God's will? Be specific.

5. Write down the names of your "wise counselors" who can help you discern if a decision you are planning to make is God's will or your own.

6. Describe a couple of recent decisions you made where you "consciously [chose] to commit all [your] life and will to Christ's care and control." How did they work out?

7. Describe a couple of recent decisions you made where you basically said, "No problem, God, I got this one." How did those work out?

8. Finally, why would you make any decisions without first seeking God's will for your life? Be honest.

PRAYER

Thank You, God, for sending us Your precious Son to die on the cross for all our sins. Thank You for giving us the opportunity to ask Him into our lives as our Lord and Savior. We come to You now asking for your power for each of us to seek Your perfect will. We love You and we want to continue to grow in Your purpose and plan for each of us. Amen.

LESSON 6

Action

Principle 3: Consciously choose to commit all my life and will to Christ's care and control.

Blessed are the meek, for they will inherit the earth. (Matthew 5:5)

Step 3: We made a decision to turn our lives and our wills over to the care of God.

Therefore, I urge you, brothers and sisters, in view of God's mercy, to offer your bodies as a living sacrifice, holy and pleasing to God—this is your true and proper worship. (Romans 12:1)

THE JOURNEY CONTINUES

Please begin your time together by reading "Course Correction, Day 44" from the *Celebrate Recovery Daily Devotional.*

In *The Journey Begins*, ACTION is all about turning our lives over to Christ. It is a one-time decision that is life changing. In the last lesson, we saw the importance of daily turning our will over to God. Now we will look at how to take the action of turning our will over to Him.

ACTION

A—Ask for God's will to be done

Trying to do things our way is what got us into recovery in the first place. Now that we've spent some time in Celebrate Recovery, we know how important it is to follow God's will. In order to thrive in recovery, we need to ask for God to reveal His will to us, and that His will would be done, even if it goes against what we would choose. We need to spend time each day in prayer asking God for His will to be done, making sure to listen for His response.

"Father, if you are willing, take this cup from me; yet not my will, but yours be done." (Luke 22:42)

"Your kingdom come, your will be done, on earth as it is in heaven." (Matthew 6:10)

Now listen, you who say, "Today or tomorrow we will go to this or that city, spend a year there, carry on business and make money." Why, you do not even know what will happen tomorrow. What is your life? You are a mist that appears for a little while and then vanishes. Instead, you ought to say, "If it is the Lord's will, we will live and do this or that." (James 4:13–15)

C—Choose to follow His will over our own

Once we know God's will, we will have to choose to follow it. This may take making day-by-day or moment-by-moment decisions. He may lead us to do something we'd rather not, but He can be trusted.

Trust in the LORD with all your heart and lean not on your own understanding; in all your ways submit to him, and he will make your paths straight. (Proverbs 3:5–6)

ACTION

Since, then, you have been raised with Christ, set your hearts on things above, where Christ is, seated at the right hand of God. Set your minds on things above, not on earthly things. (Colossians 3:1–2)

T—Trust that He has a plan for us

God wants to recycle our pain and experiences to help other people! He wants to use us to reach others. We need to daily trust that God has a plan for us. It might not always feel like it, but we can go to God's Word for reminders when we need them.

*"For I know the plans I have for you," declares the L*ORD*, "plans to prosper you and not to harm you, plans to give you hope and a future." (Jeremiah 29:11)*

For we are God's handiwork, created in Christ Jesus to do good works, which God prepared in advance for us to do. (Ephesians 2:10)

I—Invest in others by serving

Again, God wants us to serve other people. He wants to turn our pain into purpose. One way for us to know that we are changing is when we take the focus off ourselves and put it on Christ and others. Notice, this is different from the codependent behaviors we may have developed. This time, we aren't serving other people so they'll love us or because we think we have to. Now we want to give back to Jesus because He calls us to.

You, my brothers and sisters, were called to be free. But do not use your freedom to indulge the flesh; rather, serve one another humbly in love. (Galatians 5:13)

Each of you should use whatever gift you have received to serve others, as faithful stewards of God's grace in its various forms. (1 Peter 4:10)

O—Obey God's Word

When we talk about discerning God's will, finding God's plan for our lives, and learning how to serve others, we find we aren't left on our own. We have been given a way to find out directly from God what His will is for us: the Bible. We need to daily spend time in the Bible reading about what He wants for us. But we have to do more than just read: We have to apply the truth we find there to our lives!

Do not merely listen to the word, and so deceive yourselves. Do what it says. (James 1:22)

Never take your word of truth from my mouth, for I have put my hope in your laws. I will always obey your law, for ever and ever. I will walk about in freedom, for I have sought out your precepts. (Psalm 119:43–45)

N—Notice areas to put our recovery into practice

Since we have been in recovery for a while now, we have experienced amazing changes and found some victory over key areas in our lives. Now, we may find that it's time to work on new things that we didn't know about when we started Celebrate Recovery or that have revealed themselves on the journey.

Take action on those new areas. When God reveals them, face them head-on and apply the truth you have learned in Celebrate Recovery to those areas, too. We aren't looking for freedom from just one area but in all areas of our lives!

The thief comes only to steal and kill and destroy; I have come that they may have life, and have it to the full. (John 10:10)

Questions for Reflection and Discussion

1. In what areas do you need to seek God's will today? Be specific.

2. How do you know if something is God's will or your own?

3. Share about a time when you chose God's will over your own.

ACTION

4. What do you think is God's plan for your life?

5. How often do you read the Bible? Have you made a daily quiet time a habit? If not, why not?

6. What are some ways that you can act on what you are learning in God's Word?

7. Who are you serving? How can you use what you've been given to bless others?

8. How specifically can you put your recovery into practice this week?

PRAYER

Heavenly Father, please give me the power to choose Your will over my own. Please reveal Your will to me every day. Please show me through Your Word, through other people, and by answering my prayers. I ask for Your love and wisdom and guidance. Amen.

Congratulations!

Now that you have finished this first book in the second group of the Celebrate Recovery participant guides, it's time to celebrate this continued forward movement in your recovery! You might want to take a meeting to discuss how your life has already been affected by these steps. This would be a time of celebration and encouragement before moving onto the next volume. If you live in the same area, you could meet for dinner or coffee to celebrate this accomplishment.

Your Next Step

In Principle 1, you again faced your denial and were reminded of what God's power could do in your life.

For I know that good itself does not dwell in me, that is, in my sinful nature. For I have the desire to do what is good, but I cannot carry it out. (Romans 7:18)

In Principle 2, you saw how keeping your hope in God could help you maintain your sanity and give you freedom in new areas of your life.

For it is God who works in you to will and to act in order to fulfill his good purpose. (Philippians 2:13)

In Principle 3, you focused on daily turning your will over to God, asking Him to reveal His perfect will for you as well as what actions to take to stay in step with Him.

Therefore, I urge you, brothers and sisters, in view of God's mercy, to offer your bodies as a living sacrifice, holy and pleasing to God—this is your true and proper worship. (Romans 12:1)

Now as you get ready to move on to Volume 6, *Asking God to Grow My Character*, you will again take a moral inventory to help you identify any unresolved issues or expose any new issues that may have surfaced since you started Celebrate Recovery. Remember the victory you experienced when you completed an inventory during *The Journey Begins*, and lean on Jesus Christ and the other people He has placed alongside you on the road to recovery.

Asking God to Grow My Character

THE JOURNEY CONTINUES

Introduction

Let us examine our ways and test them, and let us return to the Lord. *(Lamentations 3:40)*

Welcome to the next step study in *The Journey Continues.* You are about to revisit Principle 4 and all it entails. Remember, Principle 4 says, "Openly examine and confess my faults to myself, to God, and to someone I trust." Here in Volume 6, *Asking God to Grow My Character,* you will once again dig into the work of Principle 4.

You'll begin by taking a look at what makes, and what makes you, a good sponsor and servant leader. You will look at the truth you have discovered about yourself from prior step study groups, and then you will begin a fresh, new Spiritual Inventory. There are three brand new lessons on the Inventory to help you get writing again. There's even a brand new worksheet, called "Pro's from My Inventory," designed to help you keep track of all the good things you have done and that God has done through you since starting Celebrate Recovery. If you have a copy of a past inventory, you'll want to have it close by.

This is a chance for you to dig deeper into existing recovery issues and any new issues that have arisen since completing a *The Journey Begins* group. Remember all of the victory you experienced from your initial inventory, and expect God to do great things in your life during this one, too.

In His Steps,
John Baker
Johnny Baker

LESSON 7

Sponsor

Principle 4: Openly examine and confess my hurts, hang-ups, and habits to myself, to God, and to someone I trust.

Blessed are the pure in heart, for they will see God. (Matthew 5:8)

Step 4: We made a searching and fearless moral inventory of ourselves.

Let us examine our ways and test them, and let us return to the LORD. (Lamentations 3:40)

THE JOURNEY CONTINUES

Please begin your time together by reading "The Fourth Step, Day 90" from the *Celebrate Recovery Daily Devotional*.

The road to recovery is not meant to be traveled alone. As we discovered in *The Journey Begins*, we actually needed three major relationships. First and most important is our relationship with Jesus Christ. In addition, we found that everyone needs relationships with the people in their recovery group. Last, everyone needs a relationship with a sponsor and/or accountability partner/team. Identifying a sponsor and/or accountability partner/team was especially important before beginning Principles 4 through 6, in which we worked on getting right with God, ourselves, and others.

Principle 4 is all about getting rid of our "truth decay." It's all about coming clean! Proverbs 15:14 tells us, "The discerning heart seeks knowledge, but the mouth of a fool feeds on folly."

Are you ready to feed on the truth about your life? Well then, it's time to take out the trash! That trash can get pretty heavy at times, so we learned in *The Journey Begins* that we shouldn't handle it alone. We all needed a genuine mentor, coach, or in recovery terms, a sponsor and/or an accountability partner/team.

Now that we are in *The Journey Continues*, we will find a few new facets of this lesson. First, it's time for us to step out and sponsor other people who are beginning their recovery journey. Also, we may find that we have stepped away from our sponsors or accountability partner/team and need to find new people to support us on the road to recovery. Here are some qualities to look for in the people we need to support us and to provide for the people we will help.

> On a personal note, I would strongly suggest that everyone has both a sponsor and an accountability partner/team. Why? Because if we only have one person we can turn to when temptation comes, we could be in trouble. What if we can't reach our sponsor at the moment we are fighting relapse? If we have both a sponsor and accountability partner/team, our chances of getting help increase. Also, I have seen many situations between a sponsor and the person being sponsored become a very unhealthy, dependent relationship. Remember, we are to place that dependency on Christ's power, not our sponsor's finite power.
>
> —John Baker

SPONSOR

S—Servant leader

Sponsors should not be dictators. They lead from the freedom they have experienced in living out the steps and principles.

"For even the Son of Man did not come to be served, but to serve, and to give his life as a ransom for many." (Mark 10:45)

P—Power comes from God, not from the sponsor

We need to keep our relationships healthy. As sponsors, it's important to make sure we are giving godly advice. This is why having accountability partners is such a good idea. They can help us make sure that our sponsors are doing the same with us.

So that your faith might not rest on human wisdom, but on God's power. (1 Corinthians 2:5)

O—Open to share their recovery journey

Sponsors need to be transparent. Remember, we are all works in progress. Sponsors need to be persons of integrity.

Whoever walks in integrity walks securely, but whoever takes crooked paths will be found out. (Proverbs 10:9)

> Integrity means that if our private life was suddenly exposed, we'd have no reason to be ashamed or embarrassed. Integrity means our outward life is consistent with our inner convictions.
> **—BILLY GRAHAM**

N—Nonjudgmental

Our role as a sponsor is not to judge those we sponsor, but to guide them by encouraging them and by challenging them. Sponsors need to be role models.

"Do not judge, or you too will be judged. For in the same way you judge others, you will be judged, and with the measure you use, it will be measured to you." (Matthew 7:1–2)

S—Still growing in their relationship with God

Sponsors need to be living out Principles 7 and 8 on a daily basis. We need to be active in our own recovery.

So that you may live a life worthy of the Lord and please him in every way: bearing fruit in every good work, growing in the knowledge of God. (Colossians 1:10)

O—Objectivity

Getting too close to the individuals we sponsor can be counterproductive and develop into an unhealthy, codependent relationship.

So that your daily life may win the respect of outsiders and so that you will not be dependent on anybody. (1 Thessalonians 4:12)

R—Reachable

Sponsors need to be available 24/7 for the individuals they sponsor. We need to be there when the individuals we are sponsoring are going through a crisis.

And the things you have heard me say in the presence of many witnesses entrust to reliable people who will also be qualified to teach others. (2 Timothy 2:2)

Questions for Reflection and Discussion

1. How has your sponsor helped you with a recent issue? Be specific and provide a detailed account.

SPONSOR

2. How many individuals are you currently sponsoring? And what are some of the tools you are using to help and encourage them?

3. How do you rely on God's wisdom to help you be a loving and effective sponsor? Give several examples.

4. Are you comfortable sharing your recovery journey and current struggles with those you sponsor? Are you sponsoring by example? Share some details.

5. How are you continuing to grow in your relationship with God so your own recovery will not suffer?

6. Do you share with the people you sponsor what God is showing you in your daily quiet times? Give some current examples.

7. How do you ensure your relationship with those you sponsor remains healthy and objective? How do you keep it from becoming a codependent relationship?

8. How have you been able to maintain a healthy relationship with your sponsor? Be specific.

9. How do you keep yourself available for those you sponsor who need to reach you in times of crisis? And just as importantly, how do you establish healthy boundaries with those you sponsor?

PRAYER

Dear God, thank You for our group. We want to continue to break free from our hurts, hang-ups, and habits, and continue to grow closer to You. Thank You for the leaders You have provided. Thank You that You love us all, no matter where we are in our recovery. Show me the person(s) You have prepared for me to sponsor. Help us to establish an honest and loving relationship that honors You and helps both me and those I sponsor grow stronger in You. In Jesus' name we pray, amen.

LESSON 8

Truth

Principle 4: Openly examine and confess my hurts, hang-ups, and habits to myself, to God, and to someone I trust.

Blessed are the pure in heart, for they will see God. (Matthew 5:8)

Step 4: We made a searching and fearless moral inventory of ourselves.

Let us examine our ways and test them, and let us return to the Lord. (Lamentations 3:40)

Please begin your time together by reading "A Call for Accountability, Day 107" from the *Celebrate Recovery Daily Devotional*.

In Volume 2 of *The Journey Begins*, we started the process of taking an honest and spiritual inventory. (You may have done this more than once if we have completed more than one *The Journey Begins* step study.) Now in *The Journey Continues*, we are getting ready to do the process again.

To get the most out of this lesson, have your most recent inventory (from *The Journey Begins*) available for reference.

Remember, in our inventory we write down all of the good and bad things that we have done and that have been done to us. For many of us, this can be a hard process. You may be wondering, *Why do we need to do this again? Why is this such an important part of recovery?*

Jesus says that, "Then you will know the truth and the truth will set you free" (John 8:32).

When we complete a moral inventory, we begin to see the TRUTH about ourselves. Now that we have been living out our recoveries, how do we continue to find freedom from our hurts, hang-ups, and habits that Jesus promises?

The answer lies in the truth!

TRUTH

<u>**T—Take action on any unresolved relational issues from our inventory or on any new issues that have begun**</u>

As you look over your last moral inventory, are there any issues that haven't been resolved? Is there anyone you haven't made amends to or offered forgiveness to? Remember that these unresolved relationships are hindering and hurting your recovery—they may even cause your recovery to stall. Ask yourself why you haven't taken the action you need to on these, and call your sponsor or accountability partners/team to ask for their help. Don't leave this to chance. Make a plan on how you will proceed.

> *"Therefore, if you are offering your gift at the altar and there remember that your brother or sister has something against you, leave your gift there in front of the altar. First go and be reconciled to them; then come and offer your gift." (Matthew 5:23–24)*

Bear with each other and forgive one another if any of you has a grievance against someone. Forgive as the Lord forgave you. (Colossians 3:13)

R—Recognize patterns and behaviors

One way the truth sets us free is by showing us clearly, through the process of the moral inventory, patterns that we may be able to ignore until we see them written on the page.

I do not understand what I do. For what I want to do I do not do, but what I hate I do. And if I do what I do not want to do, I agree that the law is good. As it is, it is no longer I myself who do it, but it is sin living in me. For I know that good itself does not dwell in me, that is, in my sinful nature. For I have the desire to do what is good, but I cannot carry it out. (Romans 7:15–18)

Anyone who listens to the word but does not do what it says is like someone who looks at his face in a mirror and, after looking at himself, goes away and immediately forgets what he looks like. But whoever looks intently into the perfect law that gives freedom, and continues in it—not forgetting what they have heard, but doing it—they will be blessed in what they do. (James 1:23–25)

U—Understand that the events in our past shaped us, but they don't define us

Again referencing your latest moral inventory, notice that you were shaped both positively and negatively by the events of your past.

It's in dealing with the events of the past and understanding that they had a hand in making us who we are today, that we are able to face them and then move forward. Denying their impact might feel like freedom, but until we have dealt with them honestly, we will remain trapped by them. We may have done things we regret or things may have been done to us that we wish never happened. Acknowledging their influence, but also trusting that Jesus can use them to help others, takes away their power to define us.

Therefore, there is now no condemnation for those who are in Christ Jesus. (Romans 8:1)

"I [God], even I, am he who blots out your transgressions, for my own sake, and remembers your sins no more. Review the past for me, let us argue the matter together; state the case for your innocence." (Isaiah 43:25–26)

Praise be to the God and Father of our Lord Jesus Christ, the Father of compassion and the God of all comfort, who comforts us in all our troubles, so that we can comfort those in any trouble with the comfort we ourselves receive from God. (2 Corinthians 1:3–4)

T—Turn our character defects over to Jesus

Because you are doing a *The Journey Continues* step study, you have already turned your life and at least one recovery issue over to Jesus. You have undoubtedly found freedom over some of the hurts, hang-ups, and habits in your life.

However, if we want to find complete freedom, we need to turn it *all* over to Him. As we have completed a moral inventory and have begun taking a daily inventory, we have most likely observed new character defects other than those that initially brought us to Celebrate Recovery. It is now time to turn those areas over to Jesus as well.

If we confess our sins, he is faithful and just and will forgive us our sins and purify us from all unrighteousness. (1 John 1:9)

H—Help others along the way

We find freedom when we are able to take the focus off ourselves and put it on helping others. The key in making sure we are doing this in a healthy way is by keeping Jesus at the center of our service. When we help other people, we are directly serving Christ.

Do nothing out of selfish ambition or vain conceit. Rather, in humility value others above yourselves, not looking to your own interests but each of you to the interests of the others. In your relationships with one another, have the same mindset as Christ Jesus. (Philippians 2:3–5)

Questions for Reflection and Discussion

1. As you prepare to do a new inventory, how are you feeling? Excited? Worried? Be specific.

TRUTH

2. Share a lesson you learned from a prior inventory.

3. Review the copy of your most recent inventory. Do you see any relationships or issues that have gone unresolved? If so, what actions do you need to take?

4. What patterns or behaviors did you recognize during your latest inventory? Be specific.

5. How can knowing about those patterns help you as you move forward?

6. What events of your past—both good and bad—have shaped you in big ways? And how does knowing that those events don't define you impact your recovery?

7. How have you used the events of your past to help other people?

8. What character defects have you been unwilling to turn over to Jesus?

9. How can you use what you learned about yourself through the inventory process to help others? Who do you know who needs to hear your story?

PRAYER

Heavenly Father, as we begin to complete a new inventory, help us to remember the victories You gave us when we went through The Journey Begins. We ask that You help us build on that experience and grow deeper in You and in our recoveries. In Your name, amen.

LESSON 9

Inventory

Principle 4: Openly examine and confess my hurts, hang-ups, and habits to myself, to God, and to someone I trust.

Blessed are the pure in heart, for they will see God. (Matthew 5:8)

Step 4: We made a searching and fearless moral inventory of ourselves.

*Let us examine our ways and test them, and let us return to the L%%ORD%%.
(Lamentations 3:40)*

Please begin your time together by reading "The Whole Truth, Day 91" from the *Celebrate Recovery Daily Devotional*.

Let's review: As we said in Lesson 8, it may have been several years since you actually completed your 4th Step Inventory in *The Journey Begins*. You may have discovered over the months or years since you initially completed your inventory that a new struggle or issue has surfaced. Or it may be that you left things off your initial inventory and you are now ready to face them. So it is important to revisit those inventory sheets once again!

Let's get ready to write. Remember your inventory needs to be on paper. Writing (or typing) will help you organize your thoughts and focus on recalling events that you may have repressed.

Please don't forget, you are not going through this alone. You have developed a strong support team that is here to guide you, but even more importantly, your relationship with Christ has grown significantly since you did your first inventory.

Inventory

Ephesians 4:31 tells us, "Get rid of all bitterness, rage and anger, brawling and slander, along with every form of malice."

You'll notice the inventory process is the same from Journey Begins to Journey Continues. Why? Because it works. However, there is a *brand new* worksheet called "Pro's from My Inventory" on page 63 for you to write down any victories you have won and/or service you have performed. This is so important! This will help you keep your inventory balanced and help you see all the changes Christ has made in you!

It will take you more than one page to write your inventory. You have permission to copy the "Celebrate Recovery Principle 4 Inventory Worksheet" on pages 61 and 62 and the "Pro's from My Inventory" worksheet on page 63.

Let's review each of the columns:

Column 1: "Who hurt me?"

In this column, **you list the person or institution who hurt you**. So even though this column is called The Person it can also be institutions or places. For example, you may have resentments, fears, or negative emotions toward an organization like the church, the government, or the medical establishment. Or you may have been dealing with a chronic illness that has built up resentment. While working on this list, go back as far as you can into early childhood.

Sometimes, people feel guilty listing their parents or other caregivers, but we've all been raised by imperfect people. We list them to explain and understand our history, not to assign blame. Again, list people, institutions, or places. If you get overwhelmed, back up and take it one event at a time. Pick one or two events that had the most impact on you and your life and start there. Then move on to one or two more. Pray and ask God who or what from your life needs to go in Column 1. He is faithful and will show you. Lamentations 3:22–23 tells us, "Because of the Lord's great love we are not consumed, for his compassions never fail. They are new every morning; great is your faithfulness." We are not alone in this process!

Column 2: "What happened?"

In this column, you are going to **list what happened** when the person or institution hurt you. The events or institutions. It is important to be specific about these actions. For example, you might list a parent who always told you to stop crying or told you your feelings didn't matter. Friends may have dismissed your feelings as you went through a divorce. These reflections can be painful, but God is with us every step of the way.

Isaiah 41:10 says, "So do not fear, for I am with you; do not be dismayed, for I am your God. I will strengthen you and help you; I will uphold you with my righteous right hand." It is imperative to have a sponsor and/or accountability partner supporting you as you work on this inventory. They will be there to support you as you walk through the pain, some or all of this group can be accountability partners. If you do not have one, keep looking! Your step study group is also working through the same process You can begin to build relationships with them. They will be there to support you as you walk through the pain.

Column 3: "How did you feel?"

In this column, you will **list how did this action make you feel**. It is important to acknowledge our emotions. These emotions affect what we believe, which in turn directly affects our behaviors, or habits. Many of us were taught to repress our emotions. If we cannot express how we feel, or how we were hurt, then we cannot heal. Denying our pain and emotions don't make them go away. They store up in our body, making us hurt, until we finally feel them. Try to list two to three emotions in this column. This may be hard, as many of us were taught to disconnect from our emotions at an early age. It can help to have an emotions list on hand as you work on your inventory.

Column 4: "What was the damage?"

In this column, you are going to **list what was the damage**. This includes any beliefs you might have developed as a result. Remember, how you've been hurt directly affects what you think or believe about yourself, others, or God. These beliefs are our hang-ups. For example, a belief system could be that your emotions make you a burden, or that you are unworthy of love. How did your worldview change? Did you develop mistrust for a group of people based on this particular event? Or is there a pattern of broken relationships, slander, loss of physical safety, financial loss or damaged intimacy from abusive relationships?

No matter how you have been hurt, no matter how lost you may feel, God wants to comfort you and restore you. Remember Ezekiel 34:16: "I will search for the lost and bring back the strays. I will bind up the injured and strengthen the weak, but the sleek and the strong I will destroy. I will shepherd the flock with justice."

Column 5: "What was/What is my part?"

Now it's time to see what part you have played. So far, in Columns 1-4 you have explored how you have been hurt and the impact that pain has had on your life. This is the column where we stop looking outward and we start looking inward. There are two pitfalls to avoid here, one, blaming everyone else for your behaviors and habits and taking no responsibility for your actions, and two, believing that none of the first four columns have had any impact on your choices or formed your coping mechanisms.

Ask yourself, **"What was/what is my part?"** For example, do you try to control others in an attempt to feel safe? Or do you drink, shop, or go online too much in an attempt to escape pain in your life? Also ask yourself, "Did I have a part in the action that hurt me?" If so, write out what your part was.

List all the people whom you have hurt and how you have hurt them. "Search me, God, and know my heart; test me and know my anxious thoughts. See if there is any offensive way in me, and lead me in the way everlasting" (Psalm 139:23–24).

Please note: If you have been in an abusive relationship, especially as a small child, you can find great freedom in this part of the inventory. You see that you had **NO** part, **NO** responsibility for the cause of the resentment. By simply writing the words "none" or "not guilty" in column 5, you can begin to be free from the misplaced shame and guilt you have carried with you.

Celebrate Recovery has rewritten Step 4 for those who have been sexually or physically abused:

Made a searching and fearless moral inventory of ourselves, realizing all wrongs can be forgiven. Renounce the lie that the abuse was our fault.

INVENTORY

> **Please note:** *If you have been in an abusive relationship, especially as a small child, you can find great freedom in this part of the inventory. You see that you had NO part, NO responsibility for the cause of the resentment. By simply writing the words none or not guilty in Column 5, you can begin to be free from the misplaced shame and guilt you have carried with you. When you first did your inventory, you may have left this out. You may have not wanted to face it. Maybe you physically and mentally could not. Celebrate Recovery has rewritten Step 4 for those who have been sexually or physically abused:*
>
> **Step 4:** Made a searching and fearless moral inventory of ourselves, realizing all wrongs can be forgiven. Renounce the lie that the abuse was our fault.

Before You Begin

Remember the five tools to help you prepare for your inventory:

1. Memorize Isaiah 1:18: " 'Come now, let us settle the matter,' says the Lord. 'Though your sins are like scarlet, they shall be as white as snow; though they are red as crimson, they shall be like wool.' "
2. Read the Principle 4 "Balancing the Scale" verses on page 60.
3. Keep your inventory balanced. List the good as well as the bad. This is very important! As God reveals the good things that you have done in the past, or are doing in the present, list them on the new worksheet, "Pro's from My Inventory" (page 63). You will be amazed to see the growth you have accomplished since your 4th Step Inventory in *The Journey Begins*.

   For the LORD takes delight in his people; he crowns the humble with victory. (Psalm 149:4)

4. Continue to rely on your support team.
5. Pray continuously.

Don't wait to start your new inventory. Don't believe the lie, "I already did this months or years ago. It's a waste of my time." No, it isn't! It's going to be very important as you continue your journey through Celebrate Recovery. Don't let any obstacle stand in your way!

Questions for Reflection and Discussion

The following questions are for you to share in your *The Journey Continues* group meeting. You still need to share your entire inventory with your sponsor, accountability partner/team, or a person you deem safe.

1. List two of the names (or objects) that you listed in Column 1 of your inventory. Write down a brief history about each of them.

2. Write down specifically what they did to hurt you.

3. Write down how that made you feel.

4. What damage did that action do to my belief systems, basic social, security, and/or sexual instincts?

INVENTORY

5. As a result of that action, what behaviors did I develop as a way to cope? Did I hurt them, and how?

6. Use the new "Pro's from My Inventory" worksheet (page 62) to list three victories and three areas of service you have completed since your most recent inventory in *The Journey Begins*. Write a few sentences on each of them.

PRINCIPLE 4 VERSES

Balancing the Scale

Emotion	Positive Scripture
Helpless	*Therefore, my dear friends, as you have always obeyed—not only in my presence, but now much more in my absence—continue to work out your salvation with fear and trembling, for it is God who works in you to will and to act in order to fulfill his good purpose. (Philippians 2:12–13)*
Shame	*Therefore, if anyone is in Christ, the new creation has come: The old has gone, the new is here! (2 Corinthians 5:17)*
Jealousy	*"And my God will meet all your needs according to the riches of his glory in Christ Jesus." (Philippians 4:19)*
Lonely	*So do not fear, for I am with you; do not be dismayed, for I am your God. I will strengthen you and help you; I will uphold you with my righteous right hand. (Isaiah 41:10)*
Overwhelmed	*The LORD is a refuge for the oppressed, a stronghold in times of trouble. (Psalm 9:9)*
Fear, Doubt	*Have I not commanded you? Be strong and courageous. Do not be afraid; do not be discouraged, for the LORD your God will be with you wherever you go. (Joshua 1:9)*
Melancholy, Apathy	*The LORD has done it this very day; let us rejoice today and be glad. (Psalm 118:24)*
Worry	*Cast all your anxiety on him because he cares for you. (1 Peter 5:7)*

INVENTORY

CELEBRATE RECOVERY

Principle 4 Inventory Worksheet

1. Who hurt me?	2. What happened?	3. How did you feel?
Who is the object of my resentment or fear?	What specific action did that person take that hurt me?	List any emotions that you felt.

THE JOURNEY CONTINUES

*Let us examine our ways and test them, and let us return to the L*ORD*. (Lamentations 3:40)*

4. What was the damage?	5. What was/What is my part?
What did this action make me believe is true about myself, others, or God? What damage did that action do to my basic social, security, and/or sexual instincts?	As a result of that action, what action did I take? What behaviors did I develop as a way to cope?
	What part am I responsible for?
	Who are the people I have hurt?
	How have I hurt them?

NOTE: Remember to keep your inventory balanced. In each of these areas try to look for positive things you have experienced in the past.

INVENTORY

PRO'S FROM MY INVENTORY

In the same way, let your light shine before others, that they may see your good deeds and glorify your Father in heaven. (Matthew 5:16)

For the LORD takes delight in his people; he crowns the humble with victory. (Psalm 149:4)

You, my brothers and sisters, were called to be free. But do not use your freedom to indulge the flesh; rather, serve one another humbly in love. (Galatians 5:13)

VICTORIES	SERVICE

LESSON 10

Spiritual Inventory Part 1

Principle 4: Openly examine and confess my hurts, hang-ups, and habits to myself, to God, and to someone I trust.

Blessed are the pure in heart, for they will see God. (Matthew 5:8)

Step 4: We made a searching and fearless moral inventory of ourselves.

Let us examine our ways and test them, and let us return to the LORD. (Lamentations 3:40)

Please begin your time together by reading "Growing Up, Day 89" from the *Celebrate Recovery Daily Devotional*.

Before you begin this exercise, find Lesson 10 (Volume 2) from the previous *The Journey Begins* step studies. Use it as a reference to what you wrote in your first or most recent moral inventory. This time, challenge yourself to dig deeper, to look past your main recovery issue and ask yourself some hard questions. Your first inventory was likely focused on your main recovery issue, the thing that brought you to Celebrate Recovery in the first place. Now, try to see if any secondary issues may have revealed themselves. This doesn't mean that you should ignore your primary issue or leave things off this inventory, but it does mean you should see if anything *new* needs your attention.

To help get started on your new inventory, here are some key areas that deserve examination.

Relationships

People who have hurt us

- Is there anyone who has hurt you, that you felt unable to include in your first inventory?
- Are you still holding a grudge or seeking revenge against anyone?
- Who are you unwilling to forgive?

(Note: The people who you name in these areas will go in Column 1 of your Celebrate Recovery Principle 4 Inventory Worksheet.)

Those we have hurt

The Bible says, "For all have sinned and fall short of the glory of God" (Romans 3:23). This means that we've all been hurt by others, and we have all hurt others with our actions. Remember, you don't need to go all the way back to before you began recovery. Instead, focus on issues that may have come up since your last moral inventory.

- Who has been hurt by your actions?
- Have you hurt anyone and feel like you are beyond forgiveness?
- What actions can you take to make it right?

(Note: The people who you name in these areas will go in Column 5 of your Celebrate Recovery Principle 4 Inventory Worksheet.)

SPIRITUAL INVENTORY PART 1

Priorities in life

The desires of our heart reveal what we love. "For where your treasure is, there your heart will be also" (Luke 12:34).

- What things have you put above God or His people?
- What have you held back and not turned over to Jesus?
- In what ways are you still following your will instead of God's will?

Attitude

The Bible says, "Rejoice always, pray continually, give thanks in all circumstances; for this is God's will for you in Christ Jesus" (1 Thessalonians 5:16–18).

- How do you see your circumstances today?
- Have you cultivated an "attitude of gratitude" or do you grumble and complain?
- Are you worried? Are you anxious?
- How is your temper?
- Do you use anger, intimidation, or sarcasm to manipulate people?

Integrity

- Are you the same person at church and out in the world?
- Do you pretend you have it all together?
- At the end of the day do you regret how you acted?

Questions for Reflection and Discussion

1. *Your Relationships*
   - Is there anyone from a prior moral inventory who you haven't forgiven?

- Is there anyone from a prior moral inventory to whom you have not made amends?

- What is holding you back?

- Has anyone hurt you recently? Has this person hurt you in the past? Is this a pattern?

- Who have you hurt recently?

- Did you make amends when you realized you hurt them? Did you do it promptly?

- What were your motives when you hurt them? Did you hurt them intentionally or by accident? How does that make a difference?

SPIRITUAL INVENTORY PART 1

2. *Your Priorities*
   - What's the most important thing in your life, right now? How has that changed since you started Celebrate Recovery?

   - Is there anything in your life that you haven't turned over to God's control?

   - Is there anything in your life that you're willing to compromise your morals to achieve?

   - What do you spend most of your time doing?

3. *Your Attitude*
   - What do you complain about? What are you grateful for today?

   - Do you ever compare your situation to the situations of others?

- What would your loved ones or your sponsor say is your main character trait?

- When's the last time you really lost your temper? How did you respond?

- Do you ever find yourself thinking, "This isn't fair"? What about?

4. *Your Integrity*
    - Do you ever find yourself acting differently depending on the people you are with?

    - Would others look at your life and see that you have grown since starting Celebrate Recovery?

    - Is the "you" you present online and in social media the same as the "you" in real life?

    - Does your walk match your talk? How?

LESSON 11

Spiritual Inventory Part 2

Principle 4: Openly examine and confess my hurts, hang-ups, and habits to myself, to God, and to someone I trust.

Blessed are the pure in heart, for they will see God. (Matthew 5:8)

Step 4: We made a searching and fearless moral inventory of ourselves.

Let us examine our ways and test them, and let us return to the LORD. (Lamentations 3:40)

Please begin your time together by reading "The Trouble with Grudges, Day 92" from the *Celebrate Recovery Daily Devotional*.

As in the last lesson, let's take a look at four more areas to help us write our updated moral inventory. Remember to seek God and ask Him to reveal any areas in your life that you need to turn over to Him.

Mind

Since, then, you have been raised with Christ, set your hearts on things above, where Christ is, seated at the right hand of God. Set your minds on things above, not on earthly things. (Colossians 3:1–2)

- Do you find yourself thinking about, or fantasizing about, your life before recovery?
- What do you think about most often?
- Would you say you spend more time thinking about earthly things or heavenly things?
- What negative or hurtful things are you allowing into your mind?
- Are you filling your mind with healthy things, such as Bible reading?

Body

Therefore do not let sin reign in your mortal body so that you obey its evil desires. Do not offer any part of yourself to sin as an instrument of wickedness, but rather offer yourselves to God as those who have been brought from death to life; and offer every part of yourself to him as an instrument of righteousness. (Romans 6:12–13)

Each of you should learn to control your own body in a way that is holy and honorable. (1 Thessalonians 4:4)

- What are you doing to take care of the body God has given you?
- What positive lifestyle changes have you made since starting recovery?
- Are there still ways you are mistreating your body?

SPIRITUAL INVENTORY PART 2

Family

"Choose for yourselves this day whom you will serve. . . . But as for me and my household, we will serve the LORD." (Joshua 24:15)

- How has your attitude toward your family changed since starting Celebrate Recovery?
- Have you offered forgiveness or made amends to the members of your family?
- How do you see the events of your childhood today?

Church

And let us consider how we may spur one another on toward love and good deeds, not giving up meeting together, as some are in the habit of doing, but encouraging one another—and all the more as you see the Day approaching. (Hebrews 10:24–25)

- Are you currently serving at your church?
- Are you making church attendance a priority?
- Do you ever find yourself complaining about your family's involvement at church?

Questions for Reflection and Discussion

Your Mind
- What are you filling your mind with?

- Do you read, watch, or listen to anything that is harmful?

THE JOURNEY CONTINUES

- If someone found your browser history, would you be embarrassed?

- In what ways have you filled your mind with positive things?

- What is the last Bible verse you memorized?

Your Body
- What are you doing to protect your physical health?

- Have you started any new habits that are negatively affecting your body?

- Have you started any new habits that are positively affecting your body?

- How are you honoring Christ with your body?

SPIRITUAL INVENTORY PART 2

- How have decisions you've made in the past affected your physical well-being?

Your Family
- How are you showing the love of Christ to your family?

- How has your recovery changed the way you relate to your family?

- Are there members of your family whom you have not forgiven? How is this affecting your recovery?

- How have making amends and offering forgiveness to your family members impacted your recovery?

- How are you encouraging the members of your family to find the help they need?

- Can those in your family see the changes God has made in you? How?

Your Church
- Are you serving in a local church? If so, how? If not, why not?

- What are some ways you invite your friends and family to church so they can find the healing you have found?

- When you see a problem in your church or in your Celebrate Recovery ministry, do you offer a solution or do you complain?

- How are you praying for your pastor and Celebrate Recovery leaders?

- How can you better serve Christ through your church?

Congratulations!

Congratulations on completing a brand new inventory! While it was a lot of work, you can be sure God is going to do some big things because of your dedication to see it through. As when you completed Volume 5, this is a great time to devote a meeting of celebration and acknowledgment of your hard work.

Your Next Step

While completing your new inventory, you may have discovered a few things. First, you may have noticed that you are still struggling with an old hurt, hang-up, or habit for which you thought you had found victory. Or, you may have found a new issue that you had not previously identified. It might be that certain people appeared on this inventory to whom you still need to make amends or offer forgiveness.

In any of these cases, be ready take the next steps to help you find true freedom. In Volume 7, *Honoring God by Making Repairs*, you will continue the process of doing your part to make relationships right and take a deeper look at some key areas in your life.

But before you move on, spend a few more minutes reflecting on your "Pro's from My Inventory" worksheet. Be encouraged by how, through God's guidance and your positive efforts, you have continued to grow!

You've done some great work so far; keep it up as you move forward on your recovery journey!

Honoring God by Making Repairs

THE JOURNEY CONTINUES

Introduction

So far in *The Journey Continues*, you have done some great work. You've taken a close look at any denial that may have snuck back into your life; you've also learned about what God's power and hope can do for you as well as committed to daily seek His will.

Then you completed another a spiritual inventory, listing all of the good and the bad that you've done and that's been done to you. Hopefully the questions in these participant's guides have taken you further down the road to recovery and helped you go deeper into identifying your issues and defects of character.

In this Volume, *Honoring God by Making Repairs*, you will see how continuing to confess and admit your faults will ready you to experience more victories. Then you will be able to make any new or outstanding amends and offer the forgiveness to others that you have received from Christ through His grace.

As you begin this second to last study in *The Journey Continues*, we will be praying that God will be with you as you do your part to make repairs in your relationships.

In His Steps,
John Baker
Johnny Baker

LESSON 12

Confess

Principle 4: Openly examine and confess my hurts, hang-ups, and habits to myself, to God, and to someone I trust.

Blessed are the pure in heart, for they will see God. (Matthew 5:8)

Step 5: We admitted to God, to ourselves, and to another human being the exact nature of our wrongs.

Therefore confess your sins to each other and pray for each other so that you may be healed. (James 5:16)

Please begin your time together by reading "The Fifth Step, Day 120" from the *Celebrate Recovery Daily Devotional*.

"We Admitted to God, to Ourselves"

For all have sinned and fall short of the glory of God, and all are justified freely by his grace through the redemption that came by Christ Jesus. (Romans 3:23–24)

This passage tells us that we have all have missed the mark. We all have done things for which we need God's forgiveness. We're all in the same boat. We've all sinned. We've all made poor choices. We all have hurts, hang-ups, and habits, just in different areas and degrees.

God's forgiveness takes place invisibly. What actually happens when God forgives us? How does forgiveness work?

1. God forgives instantly.
2. God forgives freely.
3. He forgives completely.

The Bible says, "Therefore, there is now no condemnation for those who are in Christ Jesus" (Romans 8:1). How great it feels to live with no condemnation, to live with the knowledge that God loves us in spite of all our faults!

"And to Someone I Trust"

God tells us that it is absolutely essential to share our moral inventory list with another person: "Confess your sins to one another and pray for each other so that you may be healed" (James 5:16).

How does this verse say we are healed? By admitting our faults to one another. Why can't we just admit our faults to God? Why must another person be involved? Because the root of our problems is relational. We lie to each other, deceive each other, and are dishonest with each other. We wear masks and pretend we have it together.

We deny our true feelings and play games largely because we believe, "If they really knew the truth about me, they wouldn't love me." We become more isolated than ever. We keep all of the junk of our past inside, and we get sick. There's a saying: We are only as sick as our secrets. The hurts, hang-ups, and habits that we try to hide end up making us sick, but "revealing your feelings is the beginning of healing."

When you risk HONESTY with another person, all of a sudden, a wonderful feeling of freedom comes into your life.

(Excerpted from *Life's Healing Choices*, John Baker, © Howard Books 2013)

CONFESS

C—Confess all our sins, both those of commission and omission

Confession means that we agree with God regarding our sins. Confession restores our fellowship. Remember, sins of commission are committed when we do the wrong thing, while sins of omission are committed when we know the right thing to do but choose not to do it.

James 4:17 clearly states what a sin of omission is: "If anyone, then, knows the good they ought to do and doesn't do it, it is sin for them."

Whoever conceals their sins does not prosper, but the one who confesses and renounces them finds mercy. (Proverbs 28:13)

O—Obey God's direction and repent

We need to "own up" to the sins we discovered in our inventory.

Therefore let us move beyond the elementary teachings about Christ and be taken forward to maturity, not laying again the foundation of repentance from acts that lead to death, and of faith in God. (Hebrews 6:1)

> We cannot ask forgiveness over and over again for our sins, and then return to our sins, expecting God to forgive us. We must turn from our practice of sin as best we know how, and turn to Christ by faith as our Lord and Savior.
> **—BILLY GRAHAM**

N—No more guilt!

We can restore our confidence and our relationships, and move on from our "rear-view mirror" way of living that keeps us looking back and second-guessing ourselves and others.

Therefore, there is now no condemnation for those who are in Christ Jesus. (Romans 8:1)

F—Face the truth

To continue moving forward in our recoveries requires honesty!

But whoever lives by the truth comes into the light, so that it may be seen plainly that what they have done has been done in the sight of God. (John 3:21)

E—Ease the pain

When we share our deepest secrets, we begin to divide the pain and the shame. The more often we share our story, the freer we become from our pasts. A healthy self-worth develops that is no longer based on the world's standards but on the truth of Jesus Christ!

If we claim to be without sin, we deceive ourselves and the truth is not in us. If we confess our sins, he is faithful and just and will forgive us our sins and purify us from all unrighteousness. (1 John 1:8–9)

When I kept silent, my bones wasted away through my groaning all day long. For day and night your hand was heavy on me; my strength was sapped as in the heat of summer. Then I acknowledged my sin to you and did not cover up my iniquity. I said, "I will confess my transgressions to the Lord. And you forgave the guilt of my sin." (Psalm 32:3–5)

S—Stop the blame

We cannot find peace and serenity if we continue to blame ourselves or others.

"How can you say to your brother, 'Let me take the speck out of your eye,' when all the time there is a plank in your own eye? You hypocrite, first take the plank out of your own eye, and then you will see clearly to remove the speck from your brother's eye." (Matthew 7:4–5)

S—Start living in Christ's truth and love

To sum up the benefits of Principle 4 in one sentence, it would be this: In confession, we open our lives to the healing, reconciling, restoring, uplifting grace of Jesus Christ who loves us in spite of ourselves.

Grace, mercy and peace from God the Father and from Jesus Christ, the Father's Son, will be with us in truth and love. (2 John 1:3)

CONFESS

Questions for Reflection and Discussion

For all have sinned and fall short of the glory of God, and all are justified freely by his grace through the redemption that came by Christ Jesus. (Romans 3:23–24)

1. How do these verses apply to your life?

2. How have they affected your daily actions?

3. Tell about a sin of omission, a time when you knew the right thing to do but chose not to do it.

Therefore, there is now no condemnation for those who are in Christ Jesus. (Romans 8:1)

4. What does this verse say about your past?

5. How has it affected your daily actions?

6. Take some time to examine your heart to see if you are inappropriately blaming anyone for mistakes you've made. List them below.

7. How did you feel after confessing your sins to God? Be specific.

8. How have your relationships improved since you started living God's truth in love?

Grace, mercy and peace from God the Father and from Jesus Christ, the Father's Son, will be with us in truth and love. (2 John 1:3)

PRAYER

Dear God, thank You for Your promise that if we confess, You will hear us and cleanse us, easing our pain and guilt that keeps us locked in the past. Thank You that You always love us, no matter what. In Jesus' name, amen.

LESSON 13

Admit

Principle 4: Openly examine and confess my hurts, hang-ups, and habits to myself, to God, and to someone I trust.

Blessed are the pure in heart, for they will see God. (Matthew 5:8)

Step 5: We admitted to God, to ourselves, and to another human being the exact nature of our wrongs.

Therefore confess your sins to each other and pray for each other so that you may be healed. (James 5:16)

Please begin your time together by reading "Feeling Alone, Day 115" from the *Celebrate Recovery Daily Devotional.*

Part of Principle 4 is sharing the full results of our moral inventory with at least one other person. For many of us, this process goes against what we have been taught. For the rest of us, there are certain things we don't mind sharing with others, but some things we want to keep to ourselves. In *The Journey Begins*, we looked at what we stand to lose and what we stand to gain when we follow God in this process.

Now we are going to remind ourselves of why this is so important. Some of us have been in recovery for a long time by now. You may even be a sponsor or a leader at Celebrate Recovery. After completing *The Journey Begins*, you may feel as if everyone expects you to have it all together. But remember what Step 5 says:

"We admitted to God, to ourselves, and to another human being the exact nature of our wrongs."

And the Bible tells us, "Therefore confess your sins to each other and pray for each other so that you may be healed" (James 5:16).

The process of admitting our faults to each other doesn't end once we've completed a step study. In fact, it is an ongoing process that leads to our healing. Let's look closely at James 5:16 to see why and how we should do this.

ADMIT

A—Accountability is necessary for healing

"Confess your sins to each other . . . so that you may be *healed*."

Notice it doesn't say "so that you may be *forgiven*." That only happens when you turn your life to Christ and CONFESS your sins to God and turn away from them. Instead, it says *healed*. Part of finding the healing we are looking for comes from accountability.

D—Don't pretend you have it all together

"Confess *your sins* to each other . . ."

You need *at least* one person with whom you are completely honest. The voice that tells you to keep it to yourself, to hide, and to convince people you are fine is a liar. Use the time you meet with your sponsor or accountability partner to be open and honest.

M—Make sure both people share

"Confess your sins to *each other* . . ."

This process is a two-way street! This is not a time for one person to listen and have the answers while the other person shares. If you are reviewing your inventory—what some people refer to as "doing a 5th Step"—it makes sense for one person to do the talking and the other to mostly listen. However, this process of meeting together, sharing, and praying for each other should be an ongoing one. So make it a *mutual* time of sharing and prayer.

Everyone—whether a first-time visitor, a Celebrate Recovery leader, or a pastor—needs this kind of relationship or their recovery will stall.

I—Intercede for each other through prayer

". . . and *pray for each other* . . ."

To intercede means to pray on behalf of another. When you meet together, pray for each other. You may have a few people you meet with regularly. In fact, that's a good idea. It might be face-to-face or over the phone, but instead of ending the conversation with, "I'll pray for you," take time to actually pray together. Then, throughout the week, lift up your accountability partner in prayer, asking God to give them the freedom they are looking for.

T—Tell others of the healing you have found

There is an important distinction to be made here: Tell others of the healing *you* have found, but *do not* reveal the secrets that have been shared with you. What your accountability partners share with you is strictly confidential.

Definitely tell other people about the changes Jesus has been making in you through Celebrate Recovery. Don't keep it to yourself! Others need to know that change is possible. Look for ways to let them know you are changing.

But he said to me, "My grace is sufficient for you, for my power is made perfect in weakness." Therefore I will boast all the more gladly about my weaknesses, so that Christ's power may rest on me. (2 Corinthians 12:9)

Questions for Reflection and Discussion

1. Who do you have in your life with whom you can be open and honest? (Remember, this person needs to be of the same gender.) How did you find this person?

2. Are you this kind of person for anyone else? Explain.

3. Share about a time an accountability partner helped you find healing.

4. How do you make sure you are completely honest with at least one other person? How do you fight the voice within that tells you complete honesty isn't safe?

5. What ways have you found to make sure this kind of sharing is a two-way street?

6. Share a few ways that praying for other people and having them pray for you has helped your recovery.

PRAYER

Take some time to share some personal prayer needs with the group and then close.

Heavenly Father, thank You for the people in this group. Thank You for sending me people I can be open and honest with. Help us find freedom over our hurts, hang-ups, and habits. Please help us with the things we just shared, and help us pray for each other this week. Amen.

LESSON
14

Ready

Principle 5: Voluntarily submit to every change God wants to make in my life and humbly ask Him to remove my character defects.

Blessed are those who hunger and thirst for righteousness, for they will be filled. (Matthew 5:6)

Step 6: We were entirely ready to have God remove all these defects of character.

Humble yourselves before the Lord, and he will lift you up. (James 4:10)

Please begin your time together by reading "The Sixth Step, Day 150" from the *Celebrate Recovery Daily Devotional.*

In some recovery material, Step 6 (Principle 5) has been referred to as the step "that separates the men from the boys!" I would also like to add, "separates the women from the girls!"

One of the reasons that Principle 5 "separates the men from the boys"—or the "women from the girls"—is because it states that we are ready to "voluntarily submit to every change God wants to make in our lives."

When we worked this principle in *The Journey Begins*, most of us were very willing to have certain character defects go away. The sooner the better! But let's face it, some defects were harder for us to give up.

So, in this lesson, we're going to take another look at those old defects of character that we may have held onto. Also, we're going to determine if we have developed any new character defects. Yes, if we've been lacking in working any part of our program, new defects of character have developed. That is especially true if we have not been going to meetings or talking to our sponsors regularly. Additionally, it's a fact that we can get so involved in sponsoring or serving others, we neglect our own recovery.

Let's look at the new acrostic for READY.

READY

R—Review and pray to see if we have allowed any old or new defects of character to enter our recovery

Use your latest inventory sheets (completed in *The Journey Continues*) and compare them to your inventory sheets from *The Journey Begins*. Notice if there are any similarities (i.e., old defects of character) on both sheets, or if new issues have begun since completing *The Journey Begins*.

Let us examine our ways and test them, and let us return to the LORD. (Lamentations 3:40)

E—Establish a plan for how we are going to allow God to help us get rid of our new defects of character

We need to make sure we share this plan with our accountability partner/team and ask for their input and prayer.

Do not those who plot evil go astray? But those who plan what is good find love and faithfulness. (Proverbs 14:22)

A—Accept the changes that God is asking to us make in our lives

Continuing to hold onto character defects is not doing us or anyone close to us any good! Change is hard, but it heals.

But he gives us more grace. That is why Scripture says: "God opposes the proud but shows favor to the humble." (James 4:6)

Humble yourselves before the Lord, and he will lift you up. (James 4:10)

D—Do replace our character defects with positive alternatives

The best way to accomplish that is one word—serve. We will discuss how to start more healthy habits in Lesson 19 of *The Journey Continues*.

"When an impure spirit comes out of a person, it goes through arid places seeking rest and does not find it. Then it says, 'I will return to the house I left.' When it arrives, it finds the house unoccupied, swept clean and put in order. Then it goes and takes with it seven other spirits more wicked than itself, and they go in and live there. And the final condition of that person is worse than the first. That is how it will be with this wicked generation." (Matthew 12:43–45)

Y—Yield to God's direction to continue growing spiritually

We will get out of *The Journey Continues* what we are willing to put into it.

Examine yourselves to see whether you are in the faith; test yourselves. Do you not realize that Christ Jesus is in you—unless, of course, you fail the test? (2 Corinthians 13:5)

Anyone who lives on milk, being still an infant, is not acquainted with the teaching about righteousness. But solid food is for the mature, who by constant use have trained themselves to distinguish good from evil. (Hebrews 5:13–14)

Questions for Reflection and Discussion

1. Since completing *The Journey Begins*, have you allowed any of your defects of character to return? If so, list them below. If not, write down how you kept them from returning. (This will help all members of your group.)

2. How are you going to allow God to help you get rid of any new defects of character that you discovered in working this lesson? Be specific.

3. What are some positive things with which you can replace a defect of character? Please be as detailed as possible. This will encourage the rest of your group.

4. List some of the tools and good habits you are currently using to grow closer to God.

5. What is the biggest struggle you are dealing with today? Share how it is affecting you as well as how you plan, with God's power, to overcome it.

PRAYER

Dear God, thank You for taking me this far in The Journey Continues. Now I pray for Your help in making me entirely ready to change all my shortcomings. Give me the strength to deal with all of my character defects that I have turned over to You, and allow me to accept all the changes You want to make in me. Help me be the person that You want me to be. My heart is open. In Your Son's name I pray, amen.

LESSON
15

Victory

Principle 5: Voluntarily submit to any and all changes God wants to make in my life and humbly ask Him to remove my character defects.

Blessed are those who hunger and thirst for righteousness, for they will be filled. (Matthew 5:6)

Step 6: We were entirely ready to have God remove all these defects of character.

Humble yourselves before the Lord, and he will lift you up. (James 4:10)

Step 7: We humbly asked Him to remove all our shortcomings.

If we confess our sins, he is faithful and just and will forgive us our sins and purify us from all unrighteousness. (1 John 1:9)

Please begin your time together by reading "The Seventh Step, Day 180" from the *Celebrate Recovery Daily Devotional*.

Since starting Celebrate Recovery, you have undoubtedly found great victory over certain areas of your life. No one is saying you're "done" or "perfect," but hopefully you are noticing some major changes. Victory can mean different things to different people. Maybe you have obtained sobriety and have found freedom in an area that previously held you captive. Maybe your reactions are changing, and you are no longer flying off the handle or responding negatively to situations. It might be that you are now able to establish clear boundaries with the people in your life.

Let's look at some ways we can identify, protect, and enjoy the victory we now have, and that is still to come.

VICTORY

V—Value small changes

One of the things that can keep us stuck in recovery is forgetting that small, steady change is the key to continued growth. We often look for overnight change—to be completely transformed all at once—instead of looking for the many small ways we are becoming different. Take the time to notice and celebrate the changes and victories God is giving you, no matter how small.

For this very reason, make every effort to add to your faith goodness; and to goodness, knowledge; and to knowledge, self-control; and to self-control, perseverance; and to perseverance, godliness; and to godliness, mutual affection; and to mutual affection, love. (2 Peter 1:5–7)

Not that I have already obtained all this, or have already arrived at my goal, but I press on to take hold of that for which Christ Jesus took hold of me. Brothers and sisters, I do not consider myself yet to have taken hold of it. But one thing I do: Forgetting what is behind and straining toward what is ahead, I press on toward the goal to win the prize for which God has called me heavenward in Christ Jesus. (Philippians 3:12–14)

I—Identify what needs attention next

When we first start Celebrate Recovery, we usually work on a major issue that is causing us pain. In fact, for those unsure about what changes they need to make, we often ask them to think about what is causing them the most trouble, *right now*. But once we have been in recovery for a while, it may seem harder to identify what we should work on next. Maybe we have found some freedom from the issue that brought us here, and now we wonder how to proceed further. That's why it's so important to repeat the process of a moral inventory.

Show me your ways, LORD, teach me your paths. Guide me in your truth and teach me, for you are God my Savior, and my hope is in you all day long. (Psalm 25:4–5)

The secret things belong to the LORD our God, but the things revealed belong to us and to our children forever, that we may follow all the words of this law. (Deuteronomy 29:29)

C—Celebrate what God has done in our lives

What do teams do after they win? They cheer! They celebrate their victory. Now that we have experienced some victory, we ought to celebrate it! When we react more positively under stress, or when we choose to pray instead of acting out, or when we notice that we are different, let's celebrate what God has done and praise Him for it!

A cheerful heart is good medicine, but a crushed spirit dries up the bones. (Proverbs 17:22)

Praise the LORD. Praise God in his sanctuary; praise him in his mighty heavens. Praise him for his acts of power; praise him for his surpassing greatness. (Psalm 150:1–2)

T—Tell someone else about our victory

When God gives you victory over a hurt, hang-up, or habit, He doesn't give it just to you, He gives it to all of us. We need to know about the victory you have found. Hearing about your change, your victory, encourages the rest of us to keep going. It lets us know that God is able to heal us, too. So, find someone you can share with. And don't worry about this coming off as bragging. You won't be bragging about what you have done but about what God has done for you!

But he said to me, "My grace is sufficient for you, for my power is made perfect in weakness." Therefore I will boast all the more gladly about my weaknesses, so that Christ's power may rest on me. (2 Corinthians 12:9)

But in your hearts revere Christ as Lord. Always be prepared to give an answer to everyone who asks you to give the reason for the hope that you have. But do this with gentleness and respect. (1 Peter 3:15)

O—One day at a time still applies, and always will

Once we have found some victory over our hurts, hang-ups, and habits, it can become tempting to think we are done, that we are completely healed. While we may have found freedom over our addictions or compulsive thoughts, we need to remain diligent so that we don't fall back into unhealthy patterns or relapse. That's one reason why we identify ourselves as "a believer who struggles with. . . ." We are one mistake, one poor choice, away from catastrophe and so, to maintain the victory we have found, and in order to find victory in new areas, we must continue to live one day at a time.

"So do not worry, saying, 'What shall we eat?' or 'What shall we drink?' or 'What shall we wear?' For the pagans run after all these things, and your heavenly Father knows that you need them. But seek first his kingdom and his righteousness, and all these things will be given to you as well. Therefore do not worry about tomorrow, for tomorrow will worry about itself. Each day has enough trouble of its own." (Matthew 6:31–34)

R—Realize there are battles still to come

The battle against our hurts, hang-ups, and habits is ongoing! While we may have found some victory, we would be foolish to think there won't be battles ahead. This is why it's so important to set aside daily time with God to prepare us for the days when we struggle.

Put on the full armor of God, so that you can take your stand against the devil's schemes. For our struggle is not against flesh and blood, but against the rulers, against the authorities, against the powers of this dark world and against the spiritual forces of evil in the heavenly realms. Therefore put on the full armor of God, so that when the day of evil comes, you may be able to stand your ground, and after you have done everything, to stand. Stand firm then, with the belt of truth buckled around your waist, with the breastplate of righteousness in place, and with your feet fitted with the readiness that comes from the gospel of peace. In addition to all this, take up the shield of faith, with which you can extinguish all the flaming arrows of the evil one. Take the helmet of salvation and the sword of the Spirit, which is the word of God. (Ephesians 6:11–17)

VICTORY

Y—You are not alone

It's tempting sometimes to feel isolated and alone. Even now, you may feel as if no one has ever gone through what you're going through. But look around your group. The people in your group are there for you. It's vital that you remain in communication with your sponsor, your accountability partner/team, and the other members of your group. When things feel too hard or when you feel like giving up, your team can surround you and hold you up! They can encourage you and keep you on track. And you can do the same for them!

Therefore, since we are surrounded by such a great cloud of witnesses, let us throw off everything that hinders and the sin that so easily entangles. And let us run with perseverance the race marked out for us. (Hebrews 12:1)

Questions for Reflection and Discussion

1. What is a major victory you have experienced in Celebrate Recovery? Share it with your group.

2. What small changes have you noticed? How have you celebrated them in the past?

3. What hurt, hang-up, or habit needs your attention next?

4. How are you celebrating what God has done for you through Celebrate Recovery? And if you've failed to celebrate the victories He has given you in the past, why do you think that is so?

5. Who can you tell about the victories you have experienced?

6. How are you still living one day at a time?

7. How do you daily put on the "armor of God"? What piece of the armor do you feel like you most need today? Why?

8. What do you do when you start to feel isolated and alone?

9. What steps can you take to help others know they are not alone?

VICTORY

PRAYER

Father, thank You for all of the victories, big and small, You have given me through Celebrate Recovery. Thank You for all of the ways I am different today. I ask You to help me see all of the ways I have changed and to trust You with the next areas You want me to work on. I can't praise You enough for what You've done. Help me find others to encourage with the victory You have given me. Amen.

LESSON 16

Amends

Principle 6: Evaluate all my relationships. Offer forgiveness to those who have hurt me and make amends for harm I've done to others, except when to do so would harm them or others.

Blessed are the merciful, for they will be shown mercy. (Matthew 5:7)

Blessed are the peacemakers, for they will be called children of God. (Matthew 5:9)

Step 8: We made a list of all persons we had harmed and became willing to make amends to them all.

Do to others as you would have them do to you. (Luke 6:31)

Please begin your time together by reading "The Eight Step, Day 210" from the *Celebrate Recovery Daily Devotional.*

Principle 6 is all about making amends. "Forgive me as I learn to forgive" sums it up pretty well.

Before we got to this principle in *The Journey Begins*, we started doing repair work on the personal side of our lives. We did this by admitting our powerlessness, turning our lives and wills over to God's care, doing our moral inventory, sharing our sins or wrongs with another, and admitting our shortcomings and asking God to remove them. But then we began to do some repair work on the relational side of our lives.

We learned that making amends is not about our past so much as it is about our future. Before we could have the healthy relationships that we desired, we needed to clean out the guilt, shame, and pain that has caused many of our past relationships to fail.

Step 8 tells us, it is time to make "a list of all persons we [have] harmed and [become] willing to make amends to them all." At this point, we are only looking for the willingness to do so, to simply identify those to whom we need to make amends or offer forgiveness.

> **Important Note**: Find the "Amends List" worksheet on page 106 of Volume 2 of *The Journey Begins* step study. Make sure you completed making your amends to all the people on your most recent list. If not, start there. Then use the new Principle 6 Worksheet found in this lesson on page 111 and ask God to show you all the outstanding and new people to whom you owe an amends since you completed *The Journey Begins*.
>
> In Column 1 of your inventory that you completed in *The Journey Continues* (your newest one), you will find the list of people you need to forgive. These are the people who have hurt you. In Column 5, you will find the list of people to whom you owe amends. Transfer these names to the Principle 6 Worksheet.

Let's look at the AMENDS acrostic that will answer these three questions:

- How do I make amends the way God tells us to?
- Who do I need to make new amends to?
- Which amends were incomplete or not done at all when I did this lesson in *The Journey Begins*?

AMENDS

A—Admit the hurt and the harm
We need to see the hurtful act for the "true harm" we did to them. We shouldn't minimize or exaggerate the harm we caused.

"They dress the wound of my people as though it were not serious. 'Peace, peace,' they say, when there is no peace." (Jeremiah 6:14)

M—Make a list
Add any new or incomplete amends that we have to make. It's very important to write them down. We can't rely on memory.

I think it is right to refresh your memory as long as I live in the tent of this body. (2 Peter 1:13)

E—Encourage one another
We do not have to do all of this on our own. It's so important to share the amends we are planning to make with our accountability partner/team or sponsor before making the actual amends to the person. Remember Principle 6: "Evaluate all my relationships. Offer forgiveness to those who have hurt me and make amends for harm I've done to others, *except when to do so would harm them or others.*"

Test me, LORD, and try me, examine my heart and my mind. (Psalm 26:2)

But encourage one another daily, as long as it is called "Today," so that none of you may be hardened by sin's deceitfulness. (Hebrews 3:13)

N—Not just for those we hurt
Making our amends, admitting our wrongs, sets us free. We no longer have to carry around the guilt of the things we have done. While we can't undo anything, we can rest knowing we are doing our part to make our relationships healthy.

Do to others as you would have them do to you. (Luke 6:31)

D—Do it at the right time
Before contacting the person to make amends, pray. Ask God for His perfect timing.

Humble yourselves, therefore, under God's mighty hand, that he may lift you up in due time. (1 Peter 5:6)

A person finds joy in giving an apt reply—and how good is a timely word! (Proverbs 15:23)

S—Start living all the promises of God—again
Celebrate that our loads have been lightened!

"Come to me, all you who are weary and burdened, and I will give you rest. Take my yoke upon you and learn from me, for I am gentle and humble in heart, and you will find rest for your souls. For my yoke is easy and my burden is light." (Matthew 11:28–30)

*The L*ORD *is trustworthy in all he promises and faithful in all he does. (Psalm 145:13)*

PRINCIPLE 6 WORKSHEET

Principle 6: Evaluate all my relationships. Offer forgiveness to those who have hurt me and make amends for harm I've done to others when possible, except when to do so would harm them or others.

Blessed are the merciful . . . Blessed are the peacemakers. (Matthew 5:7, 9)

AMENDS

Who do I need to give amends to? Name and Reason	Who do I need to forgive? Name and Reason

Questions for Reflection and Discussion

1. Why is it so important for you to not minimize or exaggerate the harm you caused when you make your amends?

2. Which do you typically do: minimize or exaggerate? Why?

3. Who are the first people you included on your Principle 6 Worksheet that you will start making your amends to? List three.

4. Principle 6 says, "Evaluate all my relationships. Offer forgiveness to those who have hurt me and make amends for harm I've done to others, *except when to do so would harm them or others*." Describe how you interpret the italicized part of Principle 6. Have you ever used it as an excuse to not make amends? Why?

5. How does making your amends help set you free?

6. How do you determine when it is the right time to make an amends?

7. How do you handle it when someone rejects your amends?

8. How can you encourage your accountability partner/team to make the amends they need to make?

9. How do you celebrate when you make an amends and it is accepted by the person you made it to?

PRAYER

Dear God, I pray for willingness—willingness to evaluate all my past and current relationships. Please show me the people I have hurt, and help me become willing to offer my amends to them. Also, God, give me Your strength to become willing to offer forgiveness to those who have hurt me. I pray for Your perfect timing for taking the action that Principle 6 calls for. I ask all these things in Your Son's name, amen.

LESSON 17

Forgiveness

Principle 6: Evaluate all my relationships. Offer forgiveness to those who have hurt me and make amends for harm I've done to others, except when to do so would harm them or others.

Blessed are the merciful, for they will be shown mercy. (Matthew 5:7)

Blessed are the peacemakers, for they will be called children of God. (Matthew 5:9)

Step 8: We made a list of all the persons we had harmed and became willing to make amends to them all.

Do to others as you would have them do to you. (Luke 6:31)

Step 9: We made direct amends to such people whenever possible, except when to do so would injure them or others.

"Therefore, if you are offering your gift at the altar and there remember that your brother or sister has something against you, leave your gift there in front of the altar. First go and be reconciled to them; then come and offer your gift." (Matthew 5:23–24)

Please begin your time together by reading "Forgiving Others, Day 65" from the *Celebrate Recovery Daily Devotional.*

In Lesson 17 of *The Journey Begins*, we looked at the three different kinds of forgiveness: God's forgiveness toward us, our need to forgive others who have hurt us, and the need to forgive ourselves for the things we have done. At first, it may have been difficult to accept or extend one or more of these areas of forgiveness. But now that we've been in recovery a while, it is likely that we have experienced both extending and being shown forgiveness, and have observed firsthand how freeing it is to let go of our resentments, anger, fears, and shame. We have done a moral inventory at least twice (once in *The Journey Begins* and now in *The Journey Continues*) and have seen many of the names from our original inventory no longer show up on our newest one.

However, there may still be some people we have yet to forgive. They may have hurt us deeply, or they may have hurt us recently. Let's look at three reasons to forgive those who have hurt us:

Reason 1: Jesus tells us to forgive others.
Reason 2: We need forgiveness from others.
Reason 3: Trust cannot be earned until forgiveness is given.

Reason 1: Jesus tells us to forgive others.

In Principle 3, we make the decision to turn our lives and our wills over to Jesus Christ. As a result, we exchange our way of doing things for His. When we turn our wills over to Jesus, we are telling Him that we will do what He tells us to. We agree that He knows best for us, and we accept that His ways will be better than our own. And Jesus tells us repeatedly to forgive those who have hurt us.

Then Peter came to Jesus and asked, "Lord, how many times shall I forgive my brother or sister who sins against me? Up to seven times?" Jesus answered, "I tell you, not seven times, but seventy-seven times." (Matthew 18:21–22)

"'Forgive us our sins, for we also forgive everyone who sins against us. And lead us not into temptation.'" (Luke 11:4)

Reason 2: We need forgiveness from others.

Remember that "all have sinned and fall short of the glory of God" (Romans 3:23), which means while we have been hurt by people, we have also hurt people. We need to model for others how we would like to be treated. If we ourselves have unforgiving hearts, when others ask us for forgiveness, we will be met with a similar attitude. Because we will need forgiveness, we ought to extend forgiveness, whether or not the other person asks for it or deserves it.

Be kind and compassionate to one another, forgiving each other, just as in Christ God forgave you. (Ephesians 4:32)

Reason 3: Trust cannot be earned until forgiveness is given.

Forgiveness and trust are not the same thing. When someone hurts us, or when we hurt other people, rebuilding trust takes time and effort. It takes progressive changes in actions and attitudes. Regaining trust will take time. Some people who have hurt us may never deserve or earn our trust—they might be unsafe for us to be around. But look back at Reason 1 again. Jesus doesn't tell us to forgive people who deserve it, but to forgive them anyway.

However, if you want to do your part in restoring relationships, if trust is going to be rebuilt, it starts with forgiving the person who harmed you. You may never forget what they did to you, but you will need to let go of it and forgive them to move forward. This is different from denial, because you aren't pretending nothing happened, but you are choosing to let it go and start the process of rebuilding trust.

If it is possible, as far as it depends on you, live at peace with everyone. (Romans 12:18)

Bear with each other and forgive one another if any of you has a grievance against someone. Forgive as the Lord forgave you. (Colossians 3:13)

Forgiveness can be hard, but it is essential to your growth. As you think about those whom you need to forgive, ask yourself if holding onto the pain of the past is helping you or hurting you. Remember that forgiveness is often an attitude of the heart. If the person you need to forgive is not safe for you to talk to directly, you may choose to write a letter you never intend to send or use the "empty chair" method. This is where you offer your forgiveness, out loud, to a chair that represents the person you are forgiving. Talk to your sponsor and accountability partners and ask for guidance and prayer on how to proceed.

Also, remember that forgiving the person who has hurt you does not make what they did acceptable. It does not let them off the hook. Instead, it gives you the freedom to finally let go of the pain they caused you.

> **Important Note:** Remember to add the names found in Column 1 of your spiritual inventory to the "Who do I need to forgive?" section of the Principle 6 Worksheet on page 111. As you complete this lesson, add any additional names as God reveals them to you. Don't forget to reference your spiritual inventory from *The Journey Begins* as well, to see if there is anyone whom that list that you have yet to forgive.

(For additional information on forgiveness, refer to pages 168–175 of *Life's Healing Choices*.)

Questions for Reflection and Discussion

1. Who do you need to forgive today? Why? What has stopped you in the past from forgiving them?

FORGIVENESS

2. Share about a time you forgave someone and how it affected your recovery.

3. Are there people you need to forgive who are unsafe for you to forgive face-to-face? If so, why and how will you forgive them?

4. Which of the three reasons for forgiving others is most important to you right now? Why?

5. Is there anyone from a previous moral inventory you have yet to forgive? List them here. Why do you think you were, or are still, unwilling to forgive them?

6. How does trust differ from forgiveness in your mind?

7. In what ways are you being controlled by your unwillingness to forgive someone else?

8. What does "living at peace with everyone" mean to you?

9. Have you ever needed forgiveness from someone you were unwilling to forgive?

PRAYER

Heavenly Father, please help me forgive the people in my life who have hurt me. I know that You have forgiven me of so much. Help me let go of the pain of the past and be free of the hurt done to me. If possible, help me do my part to make broken relationships healthy again. Amen.

LESSON 18

Grace

Principle 6: Evaluate all my relationships. Offer forgiveness to those who have hurt me and make amends for harm I've done to others, except when to do so would harm them or others.

Blessed are the merciful, for they will be shown mercy. (Matthew 5:7)

Blessed are the peacemakers, for they will be called children of God. (Matthew 5:9)

Step 9: We made direct amends to such people whenever possible, except when to do so would injure them or others.

"Therefore, if you are offering your gift at the altar and there remember that your brother or sister has something against you, leave your gift there in front of the altar. First go and be reconciled to them; then come and offer your gift." (Matthew 5:23–24)

THE JOURNEY CONTINUES

Please begin your time together by reading "The Ninth Step, Day 240" from the *Celebrate Recovery Daily Devotional.*

This is the last lesson on Principle 6. We have revisited how to evaluate all our relationships, offer forgiveness to those who have hurt us, and make amends for the harm that we have done to others, when possible, without expecting anything back.

As we grow closer to Jesus and as we grow in our recovery, we want to follow His guidance and directions. As we get to know Him better, we want to model His teachings and model His ways. We want to become more like Him. Honestly, if we are going to implement Principle 6 to the best of our ability, we need to continue to learn to model God's grace.

One of the key verses of Celebrate Recovery is 2 Corinthians 12:9–10, "But he said to me, 'My grace is sufficient for you, for my power is made perfect in weakness.' Therefore I will boast all the more gladly about my weaknesses, so that Christ's power may rest on me. That is why, for Christ's sake, I delight in weaknesses, in insults, in hardships, in persecutions, in difficulties. For when I am weak, then I am strong."

Now that we have almost completed *The Journey Continues*, it's important that we commit yet another verse to memory:

However, I consider my life worth nothing to me; my only aim is to finish the race and complete the task the Lord Jesus has given me—the task of testifying to the good news of God's grace. (Acts 20:24)

Celebrate Recovery is built on and centered in Christ's grace and love for each of us. As you know, *The Journey Continues* contains new acrostics and new verses. However, we hope you will extend us *your* grace as we determined we couldn't improve on the original GRACE acrostic found in lesson 18 of *The Journey Begins*.

Let's look at the acrostic: GRACE.

GRACE

G—God's gift

Grace cannot be bought. It is freely given by God to you and me. When we offer (give) our amends and expect nothing back, that's a gift from us to those whom we have hurt.

For all have sinned and fall short of the glory of God, and all are justified freely by his grace through the redemption that came by Christ Jesus. (Romans 3:23-24)

Therefore, with minds that are alert and fully sober, set your hope on the grace to be brought to you when Jesus Christ is revealed at his coming. (1 Peter 1:13)

R—Received by our faith

No matter how hard we may work, we cannot earn our way into heaven. Only by professing our faith in Jesus Christ as our Lord and Savior can we experience His grace and have eternal life.

For it is by grace you have been saved, through faith—and this not from yourselves, it is the gift of God—not by works, so that no one can boast. (Ephesians 2:8-9)

And be found in him, not having a righteousness of my own that comes from the law, but that which is through faith in Christ—the righteousness that comes from God on the basis of faith. (Philippians 3:9)

A—Accepted by God's love

> I don't know about you, but I know that I do not deserve God's love. But the good news is He accepts me in spite of myself! He sees all my failures and loves me anyway. And the same goes for you.
>
> **—JOHN BAKER**

But because of his great love for us, God, who is rich in mercy, made us alive with Christ even when we were dead in transgressions—it is by grace you have been saved. (Ephesians 2:4-5)

Let us then approach God's throne of grace with confidence, so that we may receive mercy and find grace to help us in our time of need. (Hebrews 4:16)

C—Christ paid the price

Jesus died on the cross so that all our sins, all our wrongs, are forgiven. He paid the price, sacrificed Himself for you and me so that we may be with Him forever.

In him we have redemption through his blood, the forgiveness of sins, in accordance with the riches of God's grace. (Ephesians 1:7)

"I do not set aside the grace of God, for if righteousness could be gained through the law, Christ died for nothing!" (Galatians 2:21)

E—Everlasting gift

Once you have accepted Jesus Christ as your Savior and Lord, God's gift of grace is forever.

May our Lord Jesus Christ himself and God our Father, who loved us and by his grace gave us eternal encouragement and good hope, encourage your hearts and strengthen you in every good deed and word. (2 Thessalonians 2:16–17)

The gospel is bearing fruit and growing throughout the whole world—just as it has been doing among you since the day you heard it and truly understood God's grace. (Colossians 1:6)

Christ did not suffer and die to offer cheap grace. Jesus did not willingly go to the cross so we could have an easy life or offer a faith built on easy-believism. As someone said, "Salvation is free, but not cheap." It cost Jesus His life.

—BILLY GRAHAM

GRACE

Questions for Reflection and Discussion

1. Grace is God's gift. Four words that change everything. What does that statement mean to you?

2. Describe how different your life would be if you had to earn God's grace.

3. John Baker said, "I don't know about you, but I know that I do not deserve God's love. But the good news is He accepts me in spite of myself! He sees all my failures and loves me anyway. And the same goes for you." How does that statement relate to your life? Be specific.

4. Put into words how knowing that Jesus died for you makes you feel. Also, how has it changed your daily life?

PRAYER

God, we stand before You as a product of Your grace. Everyone here in this group who has asked Christ into their lives is also a product of Your love. As we model Your grace, we are able to do the work that Principle 6 requires.

We close with Colossians 1:6: "The gospel is bearing fruit and growing throughout the whole world—just as it has been doing among you since the day you heard it and truly understood God's grace." Amen.

Congratulations!

Congratulations you have done some amazing work! Take some time to celebrate. Before you jump into the last volume of *The Journey Continues*, take a minute to think about all of the things you have experienced so far. It can be so tempting to just keep moving and not stop to reflect on what God has done. So take just a few minutes and thank God for all He has done for you thus far.

If you have seen new areas in which to apply the principles of recovery, thank Him for revealing them to you.

Your Next Step

If you have been reminded to do your part in restoring a relationship, ask Him for the power to do the next right thing.

If you have found others who have supported you, or as you have been supporting other people, thank Him for placing these people in your life.

If you have found freedom over any new or older hurts, hang-ups, or habits, thank Him for working in your life and setting you free.

Now, get ready for Volume 8, *Living Out the Message of Christ*!

VOLUME 8

Living Out the Message of Christ

THE JOURNEY CONTINUES

Introduction

Don't stop now!

In the final lessons of *The Journey Continues*, you will continue on the road to recovery and live out the rest of your life. This is so much more than maintenance! As in *The Journey Begins*, you'll focus on what God wants to do through you now that you've found even more victory over your hurts, hang-ups, and habits.

In the next few weeks you'll strengthen some healthy habits you began developing in *The Journey Begins*. You'll reinforce the habits of daily time spent with God through journaling, Bible reading, and prayer, as well as taking a daily inventory—and see how these habits can help you build a strong relapse prevention plan.

You'll also take a close look at what God wants to do through you to help other people find the freedom and victory you have found. By giving back to God and saying "yes" to service, you'll have the opportunity to become a Celebrate Recovery leader to help other people go through *The Journey Begins* and *The Journey Continues*.

This is an exciting time in recovery! Get ready, God is about to do some amazing things in, and through, your life as you complete *The Journey Continues*.

In His Steps,
John Baker
Johnny Baker

LESSON
19

Habits

Principle 7: Reserve a daily time with God for self-examination, Bible reading, and prayer in order to know God and His will for my life and to gain the power to follow His will.

Step 10: We continued to take personal inventory and when we were wrong, promptly admitted it.

So, if you think you are standing firm, be careful that you don't fall!
(1 Corinthians 10:12)

Please begin your time together by reading "The Tenth Step, Day 270" from the *Celebrate Recovery Daily Devotional*.

In Celebrate Recovery, we often talk about breaking bad habits. But recovery is more than stopping old, negative behaviors; it's also about starting new, healthy ones. In Principle 7, we see how we are to begin living out our lives; we "reserve a daily time with God for self-examination, Bible reading, and prayer in order to know God and His will for my life and to gain the power to follow His will."

Principle 7 is all about the daily habits we form so that we can walk in step with God for the remainder of our lives. We've done some great work in dealing with the pain in our pasts, and have continued in the process of doing our part to make our relationships healthy. Now we see how we can do what Jesus told us to do in John 15:5: " 'I am the vine; you are the branches. If you remain in me and I in you, you will bear much fruit; apart from me you can do nothing.' "

Principle 7 gives us three daily habits that help us remain in Jesus.

Habit #1: Self-examination

Search me, God, and know my heart; test me and know my anxious thoughts. See if there is any offensive way in me, and lead me in the way everlasting. (Psalm 139:23–24)

Just because we have completed an inventory doesn't mean we don't still need to examine our motives and our actions. As we will see in the next lesson, a daily inventory is vital to our continued growth. The best tool for self-examination is a journal. A journal helps us remember where we have been and to see what God is doing in our lives. It allows us to go back in time and clearly recount all of the ways we have changed.

In *The Journey Begins* you were introduced to the idea of journaling and even had a seven-day challenge to help you kick-start this habit. If you completed that exercise and kept at it, congratulations! You have undoubtedly recorded great insights and growth. You have learned things about yourself and seen things in writing that you may not have realized were true. If you were less successful in that first attempt, make this the time to get started! There are so many ways to do this daily habit. You can pick up a *Celebrate Recovery Journal*, a spiral-bound notebook, or any one of the many journaling apps available. It doesn't matter how you journal; the important thing is that you do it!

If you are struggling with this habit, go back to Lesson 19 of *The Journey Begins* for helpful tips on how to get started.

Look to the LORD and his strength; seek his face always. Remember the wonders he has done, his miracles, and the judgments he pronounced. (1 Chronicles 16:11-12)

Let us examine our ways and test them, and let us return to the LORD. (Lamentations 3:40)

Habit #2: Bible Reading

Your word is a lamp for my feet, a light on my path. (Psalm 119:105)

Going to God's Word daily is one of the most important habits any follower of Jesus can build into his or her life. The Bible has been called God's love letter to us and God's instruction manual for life. The Bible is a firsthand account of what God can do in the lives of those who trust in Him. Again, this is a habit you may have already formed. If so, keep it up. If you haven't, begin today. Start by reading for a few minutes a day and see how God speaks to you through His Word.

Just as with journaling, there are many tools to help you start, or grow in, this daily habit. You can use the *Celebrate Recovery Bible*, a different Bible, or an app like YouVersion. Again, the important thing is to make daily reading God's Word a part of your life.

But grow in the grace and knowledge of our Lord and Savior Jesus Christ. To him be glory both now and forever! Amen. (2 Peter 3:18)

I reach out for your commands, which I love, that I may meditate on your decrees. (Psalm 119:48)

Habit #3: Prayer

Devote yourselves to prayer, being watchful and thankful. (Colossians 4:2)

Many people have the wrong idea about prayer. They think praying is all about talking. They begin their time praying, asking God for His will and for His answers, and say "amen" without taking the time to listen for His response! Imagine if we treated each other like that! How would you feel if you had a friend who called you on the phone, talked for twenty minutes, and then hung up before you had a chance to speak? Chances are you wouldn't expect that friend to know you very well.

When we talk to God in prayer, we need to make sure we are giving Him time to talk back to us. Now, God may never talk audibly to you, but He may speak to you through a feeling (you sense what He wants you to do) or through leading you by His Spirit. The point is: Go to God in prayer, daily, asking Him to meet your needs, thanking Him for what He's done, and asking Him for His will. Then make sure you take the time to allow Him to speak back to you! His answer may not be immediate; He may even speak through a friend or accountability partner, so we need to continue to go to Him with an open heart and listen for His guidance.

Answer me when I call to you, my righteous God. Give me relief from my distress; have mercy on me and hear my prayer. (Psalm 4:1)

Do not be anxious about anything, but in every situation, by prayer and petition, with thanksgiving, present your requests to God. (Philippians 4:6)

I call on you, my God, for you will answer me; turn your ear to me and hear my prayer. (Psalm 17:6)

There are other habits to form that will help us live out our recovery journey and continue on the pathway Jesus has set before us, but these three habits are a good place to begin. This week, try to begin building, or continue building, these three habits into your life. As you do, take note of what God is doing in your life through these habits.

Questions for Reflection and Discussion

1. Which one of these habits is strongest in your life? How did you go about building and growing this habit?

2. Which of these habits is the weakest in your life? What steps do you need to take to build it up?

HABITS

3. Do you currently journal? If not, how will you get started? If you do journal, what are some lessons you have learned about your recovery through this habit?

4. Do you have a daily time reading God's Word? If not, how will you get started? If you do, what is the last thing God showed you through His Word?

5. Have you ever memorized a Bible verse? What's the last verse you committed to memory, and how has it been meaningful to you?

6. How often do you pray? When you pray, do you regularly slow down long enough for God to speak?

7. What's the last thing you "heard" from God? (Remember, this may not be an audible voice.)

8. How would daily implementing these habits affect your recovery?

9. Will you commit to building, or strengthening, these habits this week? Who will you ask to keep you accountable?

PRAYER

Father, thank You that Celebrate Recovery isn't just about breaking bad habits, but it's also about starting new, healthy ones. Help me this week as I continue building these habits into my life. Show me ways to journal, read my Bible, and pray more this week. I ask that these three habits would strengthen my recovery, but more importantly that they'd draw me closer to You. In Your name I pray, amen.

LESSON 20

Daily Inventory

Principle 7: Reserve a daily time with God for self-examination, Bible reading, and prayer in order to know God and His will for my life and to gain the power to follow His will.

Step 10: We continued to take personal inventory and when we were wrong, promptly admitted it.

So, if you think you are standing firm, be careful that you don't fall!
(1 Corinthians 10:12)

Please begin your time together by reading "Clear Mind, Clean Heart, Day 75" from the *Celebrate Recovery Daily Devotional*.

In this lesson, we want to focus on the first part of Principle 7, "Reserve a daily time with God for self-examination . . .".

Journaling

Hopefully, you have continued making journaling a daily habit. With this habit, you have continued to commit to recapping your day in written form—the good and the bad, the successes and the times when you made mistakes.

If for some reason, you have stopped journaling, please pray about starting it again. You may be thinking that you don't have time to journal. The truth is, you don't have time not too!

Remember the two reasons why journaling is a key part to each of our recoveries as we continue the journey:

1. When you write down areas in which you owe amends, it will help you to be aware of unhealthy patterns that may be developing. As you identify them, you can work on them with the help of Jesus Christ and your sponsor and accountability partner/team.
2. You can keep the amends you owe to a very "short list." As soon as you write down an issue, you can make a plan to promptly offer your amends. After you make the amends, you can cross it off in your journal.

Inventory

Please remember as we refocus on Step 10 and Principle 7, we continue the journey of applying what we have discovered in the first nine steps.

We humbly live daily, in reality, not denial. We have done our best to amend our past. Through God's guidance, we can make healing choices about the emotions that affect our thinking and actions. And best of all, we can start to take *action*, positive action, instead of constant *reaction* to the issues we face daily.

God has provided us with a daily checklist for our new lifestyle. It's called the "Great Commandment," and it is found in Matthew 22:37–40 where Jesus said, " 'Love the Lord your

God with all your heart . . . soul and . . . mind.' This is the first and greatest commandment. And the second is like it: 'Love your neighbor as yourself.' All the Law and the Prophets hang on these two commandments."

Step 10—"We continued to take personal inventory and when we were wrong, promptly admitted it"—does not say how often to take an inventory, but remember the three suggestions The Journey Begins offered to help us keep on the right road, God's road to recovery.

1. **Do an ongoing inventory.**

You can keep an ongoing inventory throughout the day. The best time to admit you are wrong is the exact time that you are made aware of it. Why wait?

2. **Do a daily inventory.**

At the end of each day, you can look over your daily activities, searching where you might have harmed someone or where you acted out of anger or fear. But remember to keep your daily inventory balanced by also including the things that you did right that day. After all, at this point in your recovery you are doing more things right than wrong! The best way to do this is to journal.

3. **Do a periodic inventory.**

Take a periodic inventory about every three months. Get away on a "mini retreat"! Bring your daily journal with you, and pray as you read through the last ninety days of your journal entries. Ask God to show you areas in your life that you can improve on in the next ninety days and celebrate the victories that you have made.

By continuing to take, or recommitting to an ongoing, a daily, and a periodic inventory, we can work Step 10 to the best of our abilities. With God's help, we can keep our side of the street clean.

Here are a few key verses to follow for Principle 7:

The hearts of the wise make their mouths prudent, and their lips promote instruction.
(Proverbs 16:23)

Do not let any unwholesome talk come out of your mouths, but only what is helpful for building others up according to their needs, that it may benefit those who listen.
(Ephesians 4:29)

THE JOURNEY CONTINUES

The wise in heart are called discerning, and gracious words promote instruction. (Proverbs 16:21)

Anxiety weighs down the heart, but a kind word cheers it up. (Proverbs 12:25)

If I speak in the tongues of men or of angels, but do not have love, I am only a resounding gong or a clanging cymbal. (1 Corinthians 13:1)

Step 10 Daily Action Plan

1. Continue to take an ongoing and daily inventory, and when you are wrong, promptly make your amends.
2. Summarize the events of your day in your journal.
3. Read and memorize one of the Principle 7 verses listed above.
4. Live out all the steps and principles to the best of your ability. The key verse for this lesson is Mark 14:38: " 'Watch and pray so that you do not fall into temptation. The spirit is willing, but the body is weak.' "

Questions for Reflection and Discussion

1. How are you doing with your habit of journaling? Do you journal daily? Once a week? Or not at all?

2. If you are not journaling daily, why not?

DAILY INVENTORY

3. What are some of the benefits you have received from doing an ongoing inventory?

4. What are some of the benefits you have received from doing a daily inventory?

5. What are some of the benefits you have received from doing a periodic inventory? Where do you get away to?

6. How about those you sponsor? Have you helped them learn the key differences of the three types of inventories?

PRAYER

Dear God, thank You for today. Thank You for giving me the tools to continue to work my program and live my life differently, centered in Your will. Lord, help me to make my amends promptly and ask for forgiveness. In all my relationships, help me to do my part in making them healthy and growing. In Jesus' name I pray, amen.

LESSON 21

Relapse

Principle 7: Reserve a daily time with God for self-examination, Bible reading, and prayer in order to know God and His will for my life and to gain the power to follow His will.

Step 11: We sought through prayer and meditation to improve our conscious contact with God, praying only for knowledge of His will for us and power to carry that out.

Let the message of Christ dwell among you richly. (Colossians 3:16)

THE JOURNEY CONTINUES

Please begin your time together by reading "The Eleventh Step, Day 300" from the *Celebrate Recovery Daily Devotional*.

One of the realities of recovery is that relapse is possible. In this context, we are referring to any return to an old behavior, belief, or way of thinking as a relapse.

Many think relapse is unavoidable. That is simply not true. Relapse is preventable if precautions are taken. If you have made it this far through *The Journey Continues*, you have done a great job! You have found some freedom and victory over major issues and character defects in your life. Now is the time to protect what you have obtained.

> **Important Note:** If you have relapsed, you may be feeling the desire to pull away from your group or to run away from God. Resist this temptation! Now is the time to draw close to the people in your group and to Jesus. The enemy wants you to stay stuck and to go back to your hurts, hang-ups, and habits, but Jesus wants you to be free. So, if you have relapsed and are beating yourself up, remember the words of Romans 8:1, "Therefore, there is now no condemnation for those who are in Christ Jesus"!
>
> Learn from this experience and allow God to do something new inside of you; don't allow it to push you away.
>
> —Johnny Baker

RELAPSE

How do you protect your recovery? By setting up a RELAPSE prevention plan. A good plan will allow you to:

R—Recognize your weak points

Everyone has strengths and weaknesses in his or her life. In your group, some people are further along in their recovery and some are people are not as far along. Your experiences vary greatly. Because of this, you each have unique challenges to maintaining, and growing in, your own recovery journey. Some people know they are more susceptible to relapse when they are alone, or when they are sad, or when they are angry. The key is to know when you are at your

RELAPSE

most vulnerable. Once you recognize your weak points, you will be able to protect yourself when you are triggered to act out.

And remember, just because we all have weak points doesn't mean we are doomed to relapse. Why? Because God has the power to see us through!

He gives strength to the weary and increases the power of the weak. (Isaiah 40:29)

Search me, God, and know my heart; test me and know my anxious thoughts. See if there is any offensive way in me, and lead me in the way everlasting. (Psalm 139:23–24)

E—Establish escape routes

While relapse is preventable, temptation is not. If you have taken the time to recognize your weak points, you now know when temptation is most likely to come. But being tempted to relapse isn't the same thing as actually relapsing. Temptation means it's time to put your guard up. Instead of rolling over and giving in to the impulse to act out, temptation is a call to action! When you are tempted, the first thing to do is to look for an escape route. If the temptation is there, God has also provided a way to escape it.

No temptation has overtaken you except what is common to mankind. And God is faithful; he will not let you be tempted beyond what you can bear. But when you are tempted, he will also provide a way out so that you can endure it. (1 Corinthians 10:13)

L—Listen to your support team

Your sponsor and accountability partner/team, and the members of this group, know things about you that you may not even know yourself. Have you ever had the experience of someone asking you what's wrong before you even spoke? That person knew your cues, your expressions, your body language; in short, they knew you well enough to know something was wrong. In the same way, the people in your group have been with you a long time now. They have seen your good days and bad days. If someone on your support team calls you or talks to you and says they feel you are flirting with relapse, listen to them. They may see something you are having trouble identifying.

Therefore encourage one another and build each other up, just as in fact you are doing. (1 Thessalonians 5:11)

As iron sharpens iron, so one person sharpens another. (Proverbs 27:17)

A—Acknowledge your level of risk

You may not realize it, but you might already be on the path to relapse! As discussed above, this does not mean that you must give in, but you need to be aware of your risk level. The following information, called "The Predictable Pattern of Relapse" comes from *Life's Healing Choices*:

PHASE 1: COMPLACENCY

Relapse begins when we get comfortable. We've confessed our problem, we've started dealing with it, and we've made some progress. Then we get comfortable, and one day we stop praying about it, and then we stop working at it. Our pain level has been reduced—not eliminated but reduced—and we think we can live with the reduced level of pain. We haven't thoroughly dealt with our problem, but we don't feel as desperate about it as we once did. We think we don't need to meet with our support group anymore. We don't need to work the choices anymore. We don't need to call our accountability partner anymore. And before we know it, we have become complacent.

PHASE 2: CONFUSION

In this phase we begin to rationalize and play mental games with ourselves. We say things like, "Maybe my problem really wasn't all that bad; maybe I can handle it by myself." We forget how bad it used to be. Reality becomes fuzzy and confused, and we think we can control our problems by ourselves.

PHASE 3: COMPROMISE

When we get to this phase, we go back to the place of temptation. We return to the risky situation that got us in the first place, whether it's the bar, the mall, 31 Flavors, or that "XXX" Internet site. We go back to that unsafe place like the gambler who says, "Let's go to Vegas and just see the shows." But when we place ourselves in risky situations, we'll likely make poor choices. It may begin with little things, but it won't be long before it all unravels and all the ground that's been gained is lost. That brings us to Phase 4.

RELAPSE

> ## PHASE 4: CATASTROPHE
>
> This is when we actually give in to the old hurt, old hang-up, or old habit. The hate comes back, the resentment returns, or we fall back into the old patterns of behavior. But we need to understand this: The catastrophe is not the relapse. The relapse began in Phase 1 with complacency.
>
> To avoid the catastrophe of relapse, we need to take the time to see if we fit somewhere in this pattern, and if so, take action.

Let us examine our ways and test them, and let us return to the LORD. (Lamentations 3:40)

The crucible for silver and the furnace for gold, but the LORD tests the heart. (Proverbs 17:3)

"Watch and pray so that you will not fall into temptation. The spirit is willing, but the flesh is weak." (Matthew 26:41)

P—Pray and read your Bible daily

We have already looked at prayer and Bible reading as habits that will help keep us growing, but they are essential tools for avoiding relapse as well. Prayer connects us to God; it keeps us in step with Him. Bible reading gives us insight into what God wants for us. They are essential tools in any relapse prevention plan.

In the same way, the Spirit helps us in our weakness. We do not know what we ought to pray for, but the Spirit himself intercedes for us through wordless groans. (Romans 8:26)

I will remember the deeds of the LORD; yes, I will remember your miracles of long ago. I will consider all your works and meditate on all your mighty deeds. (Psalm 77:11–12)

S—Serve others, especially the newcomers

One of the best ways to protect our recoveries is by serving other people. Remember, the way to ensure service is done in a non-codependent way is to keep our focus on Christ. Serving others, which we will discuss in detail in later lessons, protects our recoveries in several ways.

- It takes the focus off us and puts it onto other people.
- It gives our pain a purpose.
- It reminds us where we were when we first started, and shows us how far we've come.
- It gives us a way to directly serve Jesus and to thank Him for what He's done for us.

Whoever tries to keep their life will lose it, and whoever loses their life will preserve it. (Luke 17:33)

Serve wholeheartedly, as if you were serving the Lord, not people. (Ephesians 6:7)

You, my brothers and sisters, were called to be free. But do not use your freedom to indulge the flesh; rather, serve one another humbly in love. (Galatians 5:13)

E—Enjoy the victories you have been given

There is one tool for avoiding relapse that often goes unnoticed, and that is enjoying the victory we have been given. Remember, this program is called *Celebrate* Recovery! We need to enjoy the victories God has been giving us. By this point in our recovery, it is likely we have more good days than bad ones. We need to enjoy that victory! We are more likely to protect the things we enjoy and celebrate. So if we have found even small victories, we need to enjoy them!

A cheerful heart is good medicine, but a crushed spirit dries up the bones. (Proverbs 17:22)

" 'Nevertheless, I will bring health and healing to it; I will heal my people and will let them enjoy abundant peace and security.' " (Jeremiah 33:6)

Questions for Reflection and Discussion

1. How have you protected yourself from relapse in the past?

RELAPSE

2. If you have relapsed, what would you like others to learn from your experience?

3. What are some of your weak points? Be specific.

4. How do you escape temptation?

5. Who has the ability to ask you tough questions or to speak truth into your life?

6. Are you on "The Predictable Pattern of Relapse" right now? If so, where? And how will you protect your recovery in light of this discovery?

7. How has daily prayer and Bible reading strengthened your recovery?

8. Who and where are you serving today? How has serving the newcomer reminded you of what life was like when you first started recovery?

9. How are you enjoying the victories you have been given? How do you *celebrate* your recovery?

PRAYER

Heavenly Father, thank You for the victories You have given me. Help me protect them by preparing a plan to avoid relapse. Father, I don't want to go back to my old hurts, hang-ups, or habits. Help me to keep growing and moving forward, creating new, positive habits in my life. Help keep me in step with You. It's in Your name I pray, Jesus. Amen.

LESSON 22

Gratitude

Principle 7: Reserve a daily time with God for self-examination, Bible reading, and prayer in order to know God and His will for my life and to gain the power to follow His will.

Step 11: We sought through prayer and meditation to improve our conscious contact with God, praying only for knowledge of His will for us and power to carry that out.

Let the message of Christ dwell among you richly. (Colossians 3:16)

Please begin your time together by reading "Active Gratitude, Day 130" from the *Celebrate Recovery Daily Devotional*.

In Principle 7, we began to focus our attention outwardly rather than inwardly. As we continue our journey, as we continue to grow in our conscious contact with God, He begins to unfold in our lives. The way we do this, according to Principle 7, is to "reserve a daily time with God." During this time, we focus on Him by praying and meditating.

Prayer is talking to God. Meditation is listening to God on a daily basis. Meditation doesn't mean we get into some yoga-type position or murmur, "om, om, om." We simply focus on, and think about, God or a certain Scripture verse or maybe even just one or two words. This week, try to focus on just one word: *gratitude*.

By this point in our journey, we have learned to listen to God, who tells us that we have great worth. We have learned that if we start our day with Principle 7 and end it by doing our daily inventories, we can have a pretty good day—a reasonably happy day. This is one way we choose to live "one day at a time" and one way we can continue to help prevent relapse.

We have learned a great way to prevent relapse and struggles in our recoveries is by maintaining an "attitude of gratitude."

Gratitude

This week, it doesn't matter how many years of recovery we have, we all need to allow our prayers to be focused on our gratitude in four key areas of our lives: God, others, recovery growth, and church.

As always, we need to write them down on our "Gratitude List" (pages 151). If you haven't written a gratitude list in a while, feel free to go back as far as six months or even a year as you complete this new list. Continue to add new items to this list as God brings them to mind this week. (**Note:** Be sure to complete your list prior to your meeting so everyone has time to share! Your responses will be the focus of group discussion; there are no "Questions for Reflection and Discussion" this time.)

Using your gratitude list, daily living out Principle 7, making your recovery meetings a priority, and getting involved in service are the best ways to prevent relapse.

Gratitude List

Gratitude to God

Do not be anxious about anything, but in everything, by prayer and petition, with thanksgiving, present your requests to God. (Philippians 4:6)

Give thanks to the LORD for his unfailing love and his wonderful deeds for mankind. (Psalm 107:15)

What are at least two areas of your life in which you can see God's hand for which you are grateful?
1.

2.

Gratitude for others
List the individuals that God has placed in your life to walk alongside you on your road of recovery.

Let the peace of Christ rule in your hearts, since as members of one body you were called to peace. And be thankful. Let the message of Christ dwell among you richly as you teach and admonish one another with all wisdom through psalms, hymns, and songs from the Spirit, singing to God with gratitude in your hearts. (Colossians 3:15–16)

Who are you grateful for? Why? List at least two individuals.
1.

2.

Your recovery so far
The third area you can be grateful for is the months or years of your recovery.

Therefore, since we are surrounded by such a great cloud of witnesses, let us throw off everything that hinders and the sin that so easily entangles. And let us run with perseverance the race marked out for us, fixing our eyes on Jesus, the pioneer and perfecter of faith. For the joy set before him he endured the cross, scorning its shame, and sat down at the right hand of the throne of God. Consider him who endured such opposition from sinners, so that you will not grow weary and lose heart. (Hebrews 12:1–3)

What are two recent growth areas of your recovery for which you are thankful? Why?
1.

2.

Your church family
In this area, you can be grateful for your church for being a safe place and providing Celebrate Recovery.

Enter his gates with thanksgiving and his courts with praise; give thanks to him and praise his name. For the LORD is good and his love endures forever; his faithfulness continues through all generations. (Psalm 100:4–5)

GRATITUDE

What are two specific areas of your church for which you are grateful? Why?
 1.

 2.

PRAYER

Dear God, help me set aside all the hassles and noise of the world to focus on and listen just to You for the next few minutes. Help me get to know You better. Help me to better understand Your plan, Your purpose for my life. Father, help me live within today, seeking Your will and living this day as You would have me to live.

It is my prayer to have others see me as Yours, not just in my words but, more importantly, in my actions. Thank You for Your love, Your grace, and Your perfect forgiveness. Thank You for all of those You have placed in my life, for my program, my recovery, and my church family. Your will be done, not mine. In Your Son's name I pray, amen.

LESSON 23

Give

Principle 8: Yield myself to God to be used to bring this Good News to others, both by my example and by my words.

Blessed are those who are persecuted because of righteousness, for theirs is the kingdom of heaven. (Matthew 5:10)

Step 12: Having had a spiritual experience as the result of these steps, we try to carry this message to others and to practice these principles in all our affairs.

Brothers and sisters, if someone is caught in a sin, you who live by the Spirit should restore that person gently. But watch yourselves, or you also may be tempted. (Galatians 6:1)

Please begin your time together by reading "The Twelfth Step, Day 330" from the *Celebrate Recovery Daily Devotional.*

Principle 8 is all about giving. It's about living out the rest of our lives in service—service to Christ and service to others. That's what it means to "yield myself to God." It means that we start looking for ways to give back, to God and to others, what we have received. In *The Journey Begins* we looked at what it means to GIVE, but now we will look at what we have to offer to others in service.

GIVE

G—Gifts

We have each received God-given gifts. He has shaped each of us in order to serve Him and His people. In Celebrate Recovery, we all have at least two God-given gifts in common. First, He has given us the gift of His grace when we each accepted Jesus as our Lord and Savior. Second, we each have received the gift of victory over particular hurts, hang-ups, and habits. While much of our individual journeys may look very different, we have at least those two gifts in common.

But God has also gifted each of us in many unique ways. You may not feel particularly gifted, but the Bible says God has specially gifted each of us. Many books have been written about spiritual gifts. For our purposes, know two things: (1) God has gifted you, and (2) He wants you to use your gifts to help other people. We are not supposed to keep our gifts to ourselves!

We have different gifts, according to the grace given to each of us. If your gift is prophesying, then prophesy in accordance with your faith; if it is serving, then serve; if it is teaching, then teach; if it is to encourage, then give encouragement; if it is giving, then give generously; if it is to lead, do it diligently; if it is to show mercy, do it cheerfully. (Romans 12:6–8)

There are different kinds of gifts, but the same Spirit distributes them. There are different kinds of service, but the same Lord. (1 Corinthians 12:4–5)

Each of you should use whatever gift you have received to serve others, as faithful stewards of God's grace in its various forms. (1 Peter 4:10)

I—Interest

Perhaps the greatest gift we can give other people is our interest. We live in a world clamoring for our attention. Screens shout at us at every opportunity. Never has the temptation to move on to the next thing, or has the fear of missing out, been stronger. We check our social media sites looking for "likes" and "comments" and stories pointing us to the new and the now.

So when we sit down with someone and pay them attention, when we show interest in them, we are giving them something both rare and valuable. Slowing down enough to get to know the people God puts in our path—to listen and give them our time—is a powerful way to give back.

Do nothing out of selfish ambition or vain conceit. Rather, in humility value others above yourselves, not looking to your own interests but each of you to the interests of the others. (Philippians 2:3–4)

"A new command I give you: Love one another. As I have loved you, so you must love one another. By this everyone will know that you are my disciples, if you love one another." (John 13:34–35)

Keep on loving one another as brothers and sisters. (Hebrews 13:1)

V—Victories

Another great gift we can give in service is by sharing our victories. We need to remember how we felt when we first started Celebrate Recovery. Most people don't come to Celebrate Recovery for the first time on a good day. Usually people seek out recovery when they are out of options or when their pain exceeds the fear of change. If we can remember how we felt when we first started, we recall that things felt pretty bleak. Of course, your experience may be very different, but you probably never imagined the things God had in store for you when you first started.

By sharing our victories with other people, especially newcomers, we give them a great gift! We let them know that Jesus has the power to help them change and that Celebrate Recovery works! After all, why would anyone stay in a program that never helped anyone? By sharing our victory, by telling other people what Jesus has done and is still doing for us, we are telling them that God has changed us, little by little and day by day. We also are telling them that God can do it for them too!

Sing to him, sing praise to him; tell of all his wonderful acts. (Psalm 105:2)

He replied, ". . . One thing I do know. I was blind but now I see!" (John 9:25)

E—Encouragement

Encouragement goes hand-in-hand with sharing victories. When we share our victories we show people that change is possible, because it happened to us. When we meet people who are just beginning their recovery journey, or who feel like giving up, we can encourage them to keep going. We can tell them that God isn't finished with them yet.

With a simple phone call, text, or face-to-face conversation, we can give others the gift of encouragement. We can be there when they are going through hard times. We can hold them when they are hurting, and we can hold them up when they feel that they can't go on.

Being confident of this, that he who began a good work in you will carry it on to completion until the day of Christ Jesus. (Philippians 1:6)

Let the message of Christ dwell among you richly as you teach and admonish one another with all wisdom through psalms, hymns, and songs from the Spirit, singing to God with gratitude in your hearts. (Colossians 3:16)

Questions for Reflection and Discussion

As you answer the questions this week, try to think of someone you can give back to. Ask God to bring to mind someone you can serve. We have been given so much, it's time to give back.

1. Who do you know that you can give back to this week?

2. What gifts have you been given? Be specific. How can you use these gifts for others?

GIVE

3. In what ways would those around you say you're gifted?

4. How can you show interest in others?

5. Does anything keep you from showing your loved ones that you're interested in them?

6. What victory can you share with a newcomer this week?

7. Is there a new victory in your life that you have been keeping to yourself? If so, share it now.

8. Who do you know that you need to encourage? And how can you encourage them?

9. How does sharing your gifts, interests, victories, and encouragement with others give back to God? And what has been keeping you from sharing this way in the past?

PRAYER

God, You have given me so much. As I think back to what I was like when I first started Celebrate Recovery, I can barely recognize that person. I have been giving back to others already, but now I commit to take it up a notch. Please show me how I can use my gifts, my interests, my victories, and encouragement to serve other people and to give back to You. I ask You to put people that I can give back to on my path this week. It's in Your name I pray, amen.

LESSON 24

Yes

Principle 8: Yield myself to God to be used to bring this Good News to others, both by my example and by my words.

Blessed are those who are persecuted because of righteousness, for theirs is the kingdom of heaven. (Matthew 5:10)

Step 12: Having had a spiritual experience as the result of these steps, we try to carry this message to others and to practice these principles in all our affairs.

Brothers and sisters, if someone is caught in a sin, you who live by the Spirit should restore that person gently. But watch yourselves, or you also may be tempted. (Galatians 6:1)

Please begin your time together by reading "The Special Guest, Day 360" from the *Celebrate Recovery Daily Devotional.*

We have used this illustration many times, but it is still relevant today. Take an old, beat-up soda can—dirty, dented, holes in it. A few years ago, it would have been thrown in the garbage and deemed useless, of no value. Today it can be recycled, melted down, purified, and made into a new can—shiny and clean—that can be used again.

In this lesson, we are going to focus on new ways of letting God recycle our pain by allowing God's fire and light to shine on it, to melt down our old hurts, hang-ups, and habits so they can be used again in a positive way.

By working through the steps and principles in *The Journey Begins*, we learned that pain has value, as do the people who experience it. Remember, our brokenness is not useless. God can always use your pain to build a stronger you!

Principle 8 states, "Yield myself to God to be used to bring this Good News to others, both by my example and by my words." To truly practice this principle, we must give God the latitude to use us as He sees fit. We do that by presenting everything we have—our time, talents, and treasures—to Him. We hold loosely all that we call our own, recognizing that all of it comes from His hand.

Our acrostic couldn't be any more positive! It is the word YES.

YES

Y—Yield myself to God and to the service of others

That's what Principle 8 is all about. God has created and gifted each of us with a unique purpose. His purpose, His plan, for us is perfect. All we have to do is to yield ourselves to His will for us.

Then Jesus said to his disciples, "Whoever wants to be my disciple must deny themselves and take up their cross and follow me." (Matthew 16:24)

Let us hold unswervingly to the hope we profess, for he who promised is faithful. And let us consider how we may spur one another on toward love and good deeds. (Hebrews 10:23–24)

E—Example is what is important to others

Do they see Christ in you? We must be doers of the Word. We must have a message worth remembering, a lifestyle worth considering, and a faith worth imitating.

Do not merely listen to the word, and so deceive yourselves. Do what it says. (James 1:22)

Follow my example, as I follow the example of Christ. (1 Corinthians 11:1)

S—Serve others as Jesus Christ did by finding new ways to help them

We need to use new tools and ways to reach the next generation. But God's message must remain constant and undiluted.

But now, by dying to what once bound us, we have been released from the law so that we serve in the new way of the Spirit, and not in the old way of the written code. (Romans 7:6)

There are different kinds of gifts, but the same Spirit distributes them. There are different kinds of service, but the same Lord. (1 Corinthians 12:4–5)

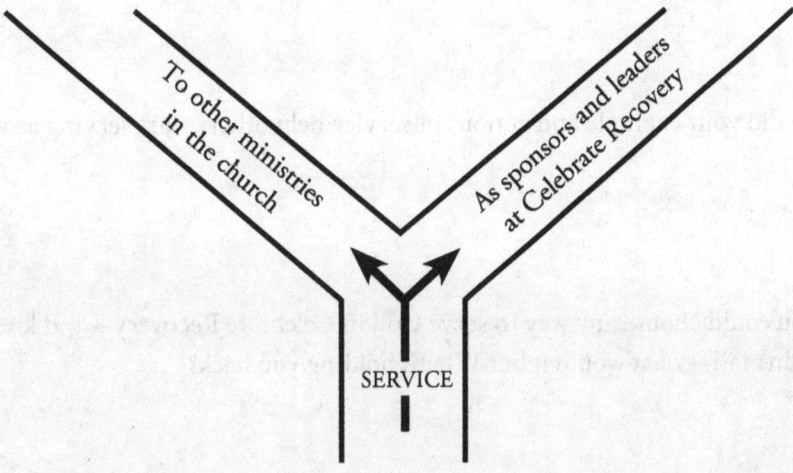

The road to recovery leads to service. When you reach Principle 8, the road splits. Most of you will choose to serve at Celebrate Recovery. Others will choose to serve in other areas of the church. The fact is, both are important.

The greatest need is for you to share your experiences, strengths, and hopes with newcomers at Celebrate Recovery. You do that as leaders, sponsors, and accountability partners. But the church also needs your service. As you serve outside of Celebrate Recovery, you can share with others and encourage them to get them into recovery when they are ready to work on their hurts, hang-ups, and habits.

Questions for Reflection and Discussion

1. In Celebrate Recovery, what areas have you served in? List the dates.

2. From the above list, what were your two most fulfilling and fruitful areas of service? Why?

3. How did your example and actions of service help others start serving as well?

4. If you could choose any way to serve God in Celebrate Recovery—and knew you wouldn't fail—what would it be? What's holding you back?

5. What are some new ways you could reach out to get more newcomers to attend Celebrate Recovery? Be specific.

6. If you are not currently giving back by serving, what's stopping you?

PRAYER

Dear Jesus, as it would please You, bring me someone today whom I can serve. Please continue to help me daily choose to make my life a mission, not an intermission. Amen.

If you will pray this prayer every morning, watch how God will use you in ways you never thought possible!

LESSON 25

Leader

Please begin your time together by reading "Serving Others, Day 302" from the *Celebrate Recovery Daily Devotional*.

In order for Celebrate Recovery to grow and in order for us to "bring this Good News to others," it is important that you become a leader. You have had at least two great leaders, one for this group and one for your *The Journey Begins* step study. Because they stepped across the line and decided to give back by becoming leaders, you had the opportunity to attend these groups. Now it's your turn.

But you might be saying, "Who? Me? I'm not a leader!" That's where you're wrong. It doesn't take a superhero to be a leader. So what are the qualities of a great Celebrate Recovery leader?

LEADER

Celebrate Recovery leaders are:

L—Learners

You may have heard the statement, "Leaders are learners." It's true. Great leaders never stop learning. Think about all of the things you have learned about God and yourself during your time in Celebrate Recovery! You are a learner! To continue in the process of learning, you now have the opportunity to repeat the process, as a leader of *The Journey Begins* and eventually *The Journey Continues*. You can help others learn about themselves, all the while learning even more about yourself. Many people have completed multiple step studies as leaders, and each of them has learned more about themselves in each successive study.

Choose my instruction instead of silver, knowledge rather than choice gold. (Proverbs 8:10)

Apply your heart to instruction and your ears to words of knowledge. (Proverbs 23:12)

E—Encouragers

One of the key roles leaders play is that of encourager. From time to time, a leader will be called on to encourage others to stay on the path of recovery or to take the next step to go further down that road. You don't have to be a cheerleader to encourage people; an authentic word spoken out of love will mean so much more.

Anxiety weighs down the heart, but a kind word cheers it up. (Proverbs 12:25)

Therefore encourage one another and build each other up, just as in fact you are doing. (1 Thessalonians 5:11)

A—Available

Here's some good news: Leaders aren't perfect; they are just available. To be a great leader, you don't have to have it all together. Because you are now completing at least your second step study, you have been in recovery a long time, and have experiences and victories to draw on that are invaluable for new participants. You don't have to have all the answers; all you have to be is available. Leaders are available to lead groups, but they are also available to have conversations—in person and over the phone—with the people they are serving. Of course, you don't have to be available all the time; that's one reason we have coleaders in the groups.

Every day they continued to meet together in the temple courts. They broke bread in their homes and ate together with glad and sincere hearts. (Acts 2:46)

Glorify the LORD with me; let us exalt his name together. (Psalm 34:3)

D—Dependable

One of the key qualities of a leader is dependability. Leaders need to be people others can count on. That *doesn't* mean leaders are responsible for others' doing the right thing or that they need to fix people. It *does* mean that they need to do what they say they are going to do. Our walks need to match our talks. When a leader promises to be somewhere, he or she needs to be there. Each week, the group is depending on the leader being present. That's not to say a leader can't miss a week now and then, but he or she needs to be there most of the time, especially for the newcomer.

And as for you, brothers and sisters, never tire of doing what is good. (2 Thessalonians 3:13)

Let us not become weary in doing good, for at the proper time we will reap a harvest if we do not give up. (Galatians 6:9)

"But as for you, be strong and do not give up, for your work will be rewarded." (2 Chronicles 15:7)

E—Examples

What is the best way to lead? By example. Great leaders don't tell people what to do; they show them. The best way to lead by example is to share what you have learned. That means that leaders share and follow the small group guidelines during group. Yes, we share about the victories, freedom, and hope we have found, but we are also real and open about our current struggles. By sharing in this way, we will set the example for everyone else.

Remember your leaders, who spoke the word of God to you. Consider the outcome of their way of life and imitate their faith. (Hebrews 13:7)

"Now that I, your Lord and Teacher, have washed your feet, you also should wash one another's feet. I have set you an example that you should do as I have done for you." (John 13:14–15)

Don't let anyone look down on you because you are young, but set an example for the believers in speech, in conduct, in love, in faith and in purity. (1 Timothy 4:12)

R—Relational

Leading in Celebrate Recovery is all about relationships. It's been said that "people don't care about how much you know until they know how much you care." Although leaders do have other roles, their main job is to love people. Get to know the people in your group. Learn their names; spend time with them; be open and honest with them. All of the other attributes of a leader are wrapped up into this one. This doesn't mean you have to be an extrovert or that you have to know everyone; God uses each of us differently, but loving people is a must!

In your relationships with one another, have the same mindset as Christ Jesus. (Philippians 2:5)

Jesus replied: " 'Love the Lord your God with all your heart and with all your soul and with all your mind.' This is the first and greatest commandment. And the second is like it: 'Love your neighbor as yourself.' All the Law and the Prophets hang on these two commandments." (Matthew 22:37-40)

And let us consider how we may spur one another on toward love and good deeds, not giving up meeting together, as some are in the habit of doing, but encouraging one another—and all the more as you see the Day approaching. (Hebrews 10:24-25)

The need for new leaders to lead open-share groups and step study groups has never been greater! It is so exciting that God is going to allow us to double the amount of step study groups with *The Journey Continues*. But that can only happen if you step across the line and become a leader, to give the same opportunities to others that you were given.

Questions for Reflection and Discussion

1. Are you ready to become a Celebrate Recovery leader? If not, what's holding you back? If yes, what steps do you need to take next?

LEADER

2. Which qualities of a leader do you feel you are strongest in? How did you become strong in that area?

3. Which qualities of a leader do you see as your weakest areas? What will you do to grow in those areas?

4. What is the last lesson you learned about yourself in Celebrate Recovery? Be specific.

5. How do you show encouragement to others?

6. How do you show others you are available for them?

7. What does being a dependable leader mean to you?

8. How can you share from your experience, strength, and hope to help the people in your group?

9. What does the statement "People don't care how much you know until they know how much you care" mean to you?

10. If you are already a leader, share about the greatest joy you have experienced as a leader.

PRAYER

Heavenly Father, thank You for all of the changes You have made in me. Thank You for the people and experiences You have given me in Celebrate Recovery. Now I ask You to help me give back to others in service as a leader. Show me the steps I need to take to become a Celebrate Recovery leader and help me as I take on this commitment. Thank You for placing me in a ministry that allows me to give back to You and others. In Your name I pray, amen.

Congratulations!

Congratulations! You have now completed *The Journey Continues*, **take time to celebrate this achievement and thank God for all of the things He revealed to you during this study. We hope you have learned more about yourself; found victory over your hurts, hang-ups, and habits; and, most importantly, grown closer to Jesus as a result of this study.**

Your Next Step

So what's next? There are three options. First, you can step up and lead a group of participants through the step studies you have completed. The second option is to serve in your local church. Whether you serve in Celebrate Recovery or in another ministry is up to you, but don't miss out on the opportunity of giving back to others. The third option is to go back and do another study for yourself. If you feel that you need some more time exploring your hurts, hang-ups, and habits, you may want to repeat *The Journey Continues*. All three options are win–win!

One last thing: People need to hear your story! While Celebrate Recovery is an anonymous and confidential program, each of us needs to take the courageous next step of telling others about what Jesus has done for us. That means breaking our own, but no one else's, anonymity by sharing our stories. Prayerfully consider how you can invite others to attend Celebrate Recovery with you and how you can help them begin their own recovery journey.

Here is one final acrostic to help you stay focused on the JOURNEY. By applying this acrostic daily, you will keep the journey alive!

The JOURNEY Continues

J—Jesus is the Leader

The LORD makes firm the steps of the one who delights in him; though he may stumble, he will not fall, for the LORD upholds him with his hand. (Psalm 37:23–24)

O—Open your heart and mind to continue to seek and follow God's will

Teach me to do your will, for you are my God; may your good Spirit lead me on level ground. (Psalm 143:10)

U—Unite with others continuously. This journey is not meant to be traveled alone

Therefore if you have any encouragement from being united with Christ, if any comfort from his love, if any common sharing in the Spirit, if any tenderness and compassion, then make my joy complete by being like-minded, having the same love, being one in spirit and of one mind. Do nothing out of selfish ambition or vain conceit. Rather, in humility value others above yourselves, not looking to your own interests but each of you to the interests of the others. (Philippians 2:1–4)

R—Remember your victories, but do not rest on them

But thanks be to God! He gives us the victory through our Lord Jesus Christ. Therefore, my dear brothers and sisters, stand firm. Let nothing move you. Always give yourselves fully to the work of the Lord, because you know that your labor in the Lord is not in vain. (1 Corinthians 15:57–58)

N—Need to continue living daily in Principles 7 and 8

Being confident of this, that he who began a good work in you will carry it on to completion until the day of Christ Jesus. (Philippians 1:6)

E—Encourage others by serving, especially the newcomer

But encourage one another daily, as long as it is called "Today," so that none of you may be hardened by sin's deceitfulness. (Hebrews 3:13)

CONGRATULATIONS!

Y—You will continue to grow in Christ to become more Christlike

Neither do people light a lamp and put it under a bowl. Instead they put it on its stand, and it gives light to everyone in the house. In the same way, let your light shine before others, that they may see your good deeds and glorify your Father in heaven. (Matthew 5:15–16)

In His Steps,
John Baker
Johnny Baker

www.ingramcontent.com/pod-product-compliance
Lightning Source LLC
Chambersburg PA
CBHW011820220426
43665CB00025B/2906